WHAT IS MEIOSIS?

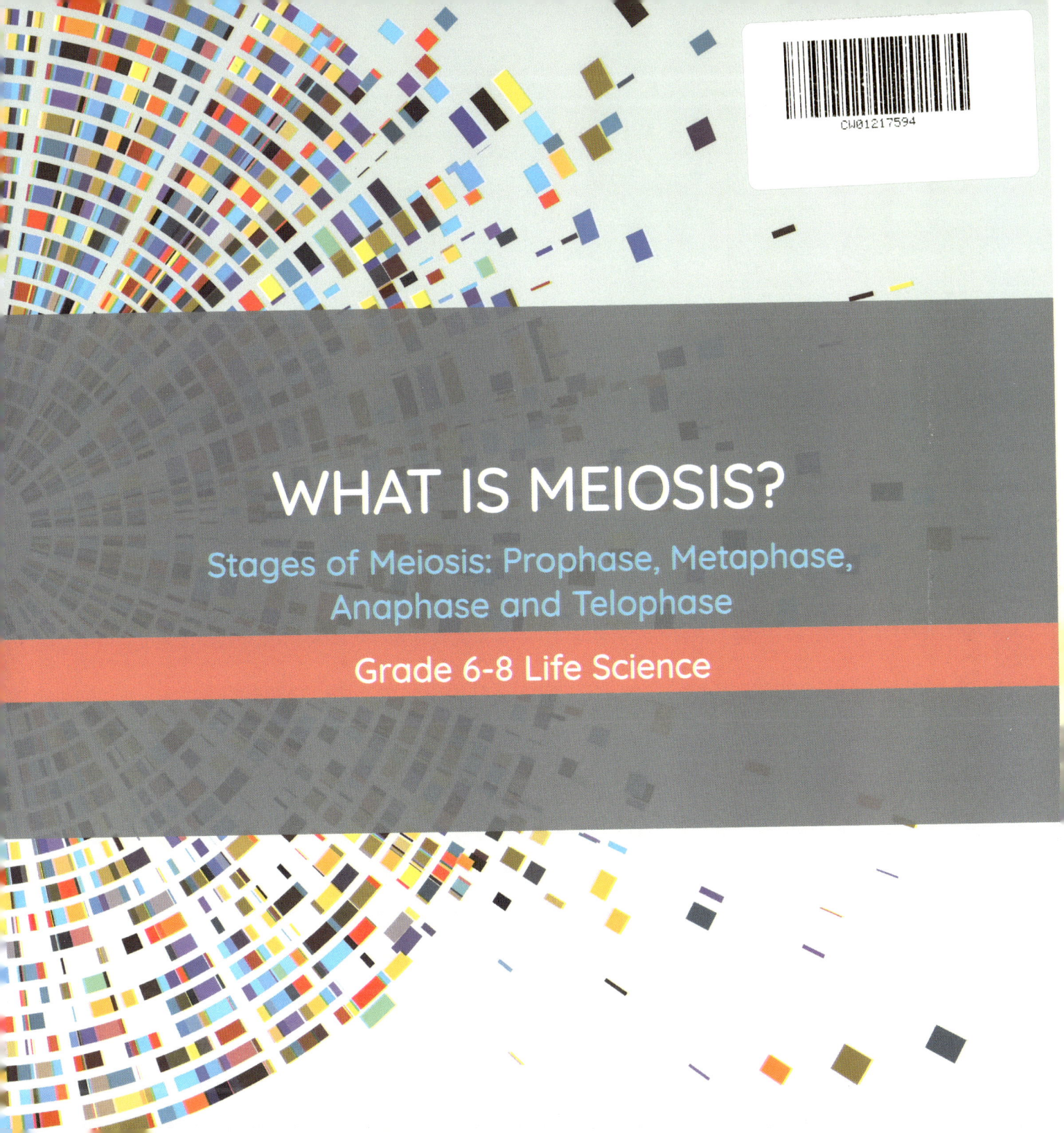

Stages of Meiosis: Prophase, Metaphase, Anaphase and Telophase

Grade 6-8 Life Science

BABY PROFESSOR
EDUCATION KIDS

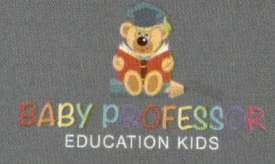

First Edition, 2024

Published in the United States by Speedy Publishing LLC, 40 E Main Street, Newark, Delaware 19711 USA.

© 2024 Baby Professor Books, an imprint of Speedy Publishing LLC

All rights reserved.

Without limiting the rights under the copyright reserved above, no part of this publication may be reproduced, stored in or introduced into a retrieval system, or transmitted, in any form, or by any means (electronic, mechanical, photocopying, recording, or otherwise), without the prior written permission of the copyright owner.

All images in this book have been reproduced with the knowledge and prior consent of the artists concerned, and no responsibility is accepted by producer, publisher, or printer for any infringement of copyright or otherwise arising from the contents of this publication.

Baby Professor Books are available at special discounts when purchased in bulk for industrial and sales-promotional use. For details contact our Special Sales Team at Speedy Publishing LLC, 40 E Main Street, Newark, Delaware 19711 USA. Telephone (888) 248-4521 Fax: (210) 519-4043.

10 9 8 7 6 * 5 4 3 2 1

Print Edition: 9781541990982
Digital Edition: 9781541992283
Hardcover Edition: 9781541998032

See the world in pictures. Build your knowledge in style.
www.speedypublishing.com

TABLE OF CONTENTS

Chapter 1
    Mitosis and Meiosis..7
    Somatic Cells and Gametes...12

Chapter 2
    The Stages of Meiosis 21
    Stage One:..24
    Prophase I..24
    Metaphase I...28
    Anaphase I...29
    Telophase I..30
    Stage Two..32
    Prophase II...32
    Metaphase II 34
    Anaphase II 35
    Telophase II...36

Chapter Three
    Sexual Reproduction..39
    Asexual Reproduction..54
    Advantages and Disadvantages of Sexual and
    Asexual Reproduction..60
    Bonus Content..64
    Punnett Squares...64

DNA double helix molecules and chromosomes

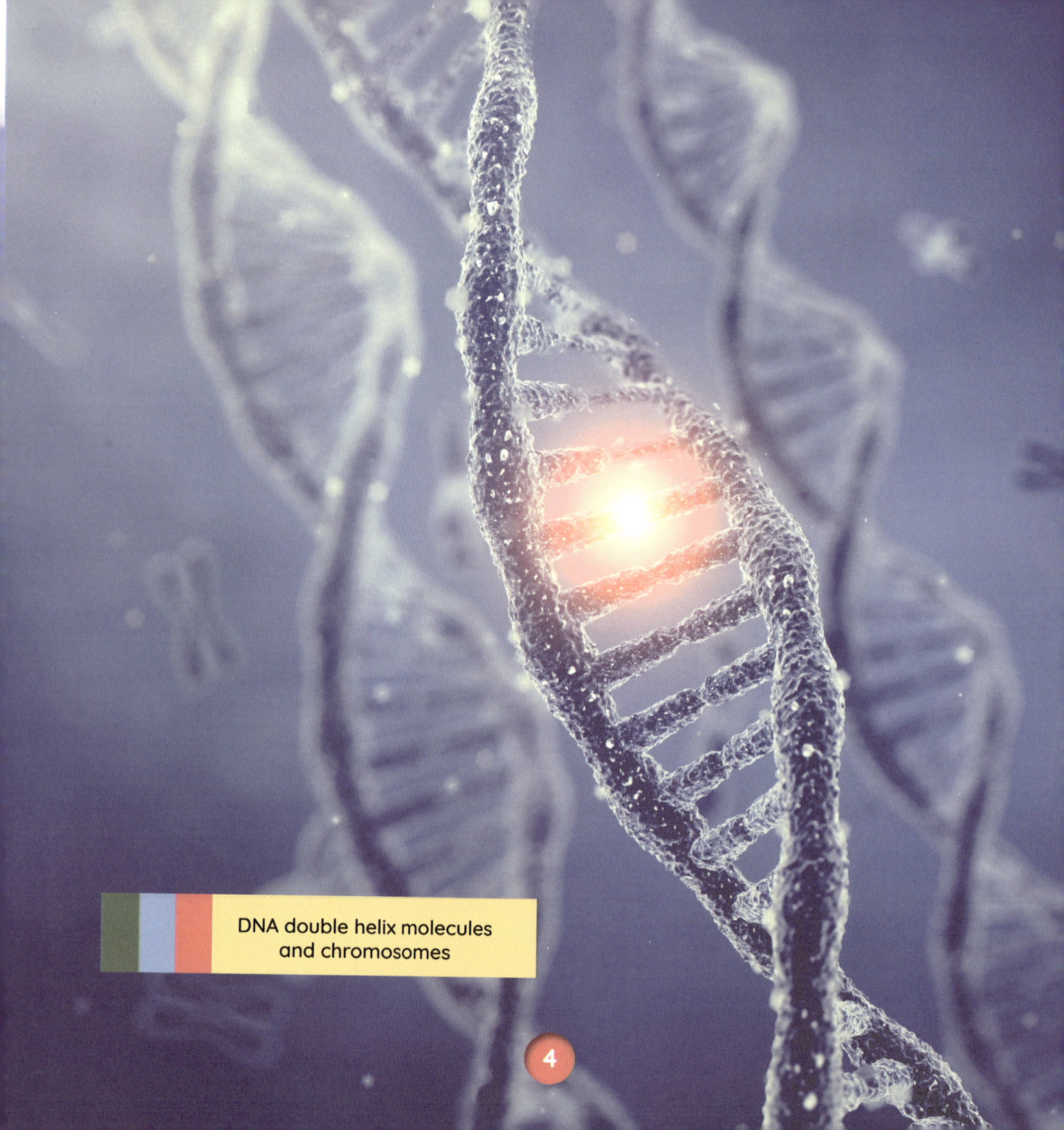

One thing organisms have in common is that they grow. They mature and they reproduce. Reproduction means to have offspring. This is what your parents did when they had you. Growing requires a process called mitosis. This is when cells divide. More cells result in a bigger organism. Reproduction also involves cell division. For sexual reproduction, a special kind of cell division must occur. It is called meiosis. This book will explain how meiosis is different from mitosis, the stages of meiosis, and why meiosis is needed for sexual reproduction.

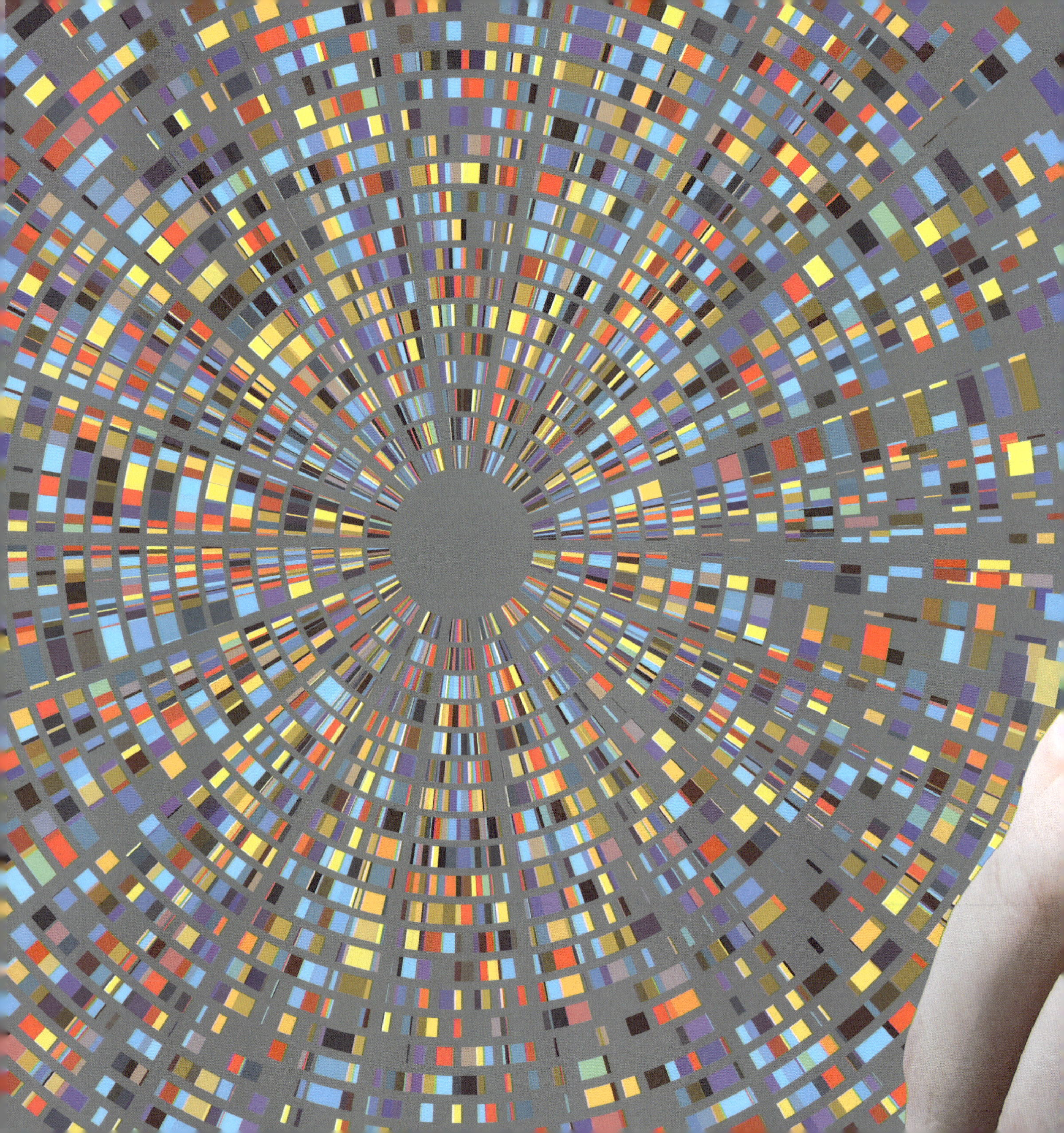

CHAPTER 1

Mitosis and Meiosis

Mitosis is the second part of the cell cycle. Before it begins, the DNA in the nucleus must be replicated in interphase. This is the first part of the cell cycle. Most of a cell's life is spent in this phase.

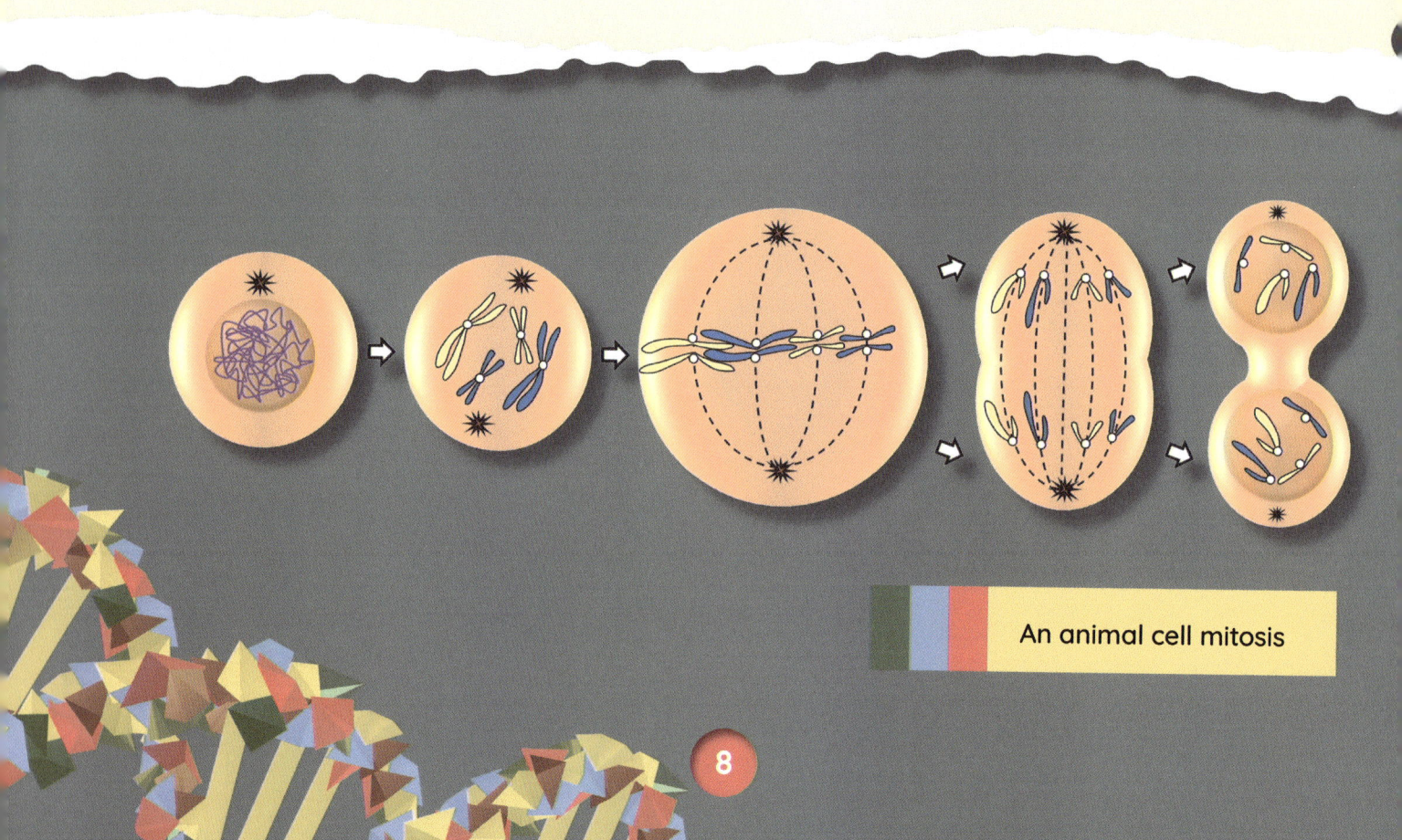

An animal cell mitosis

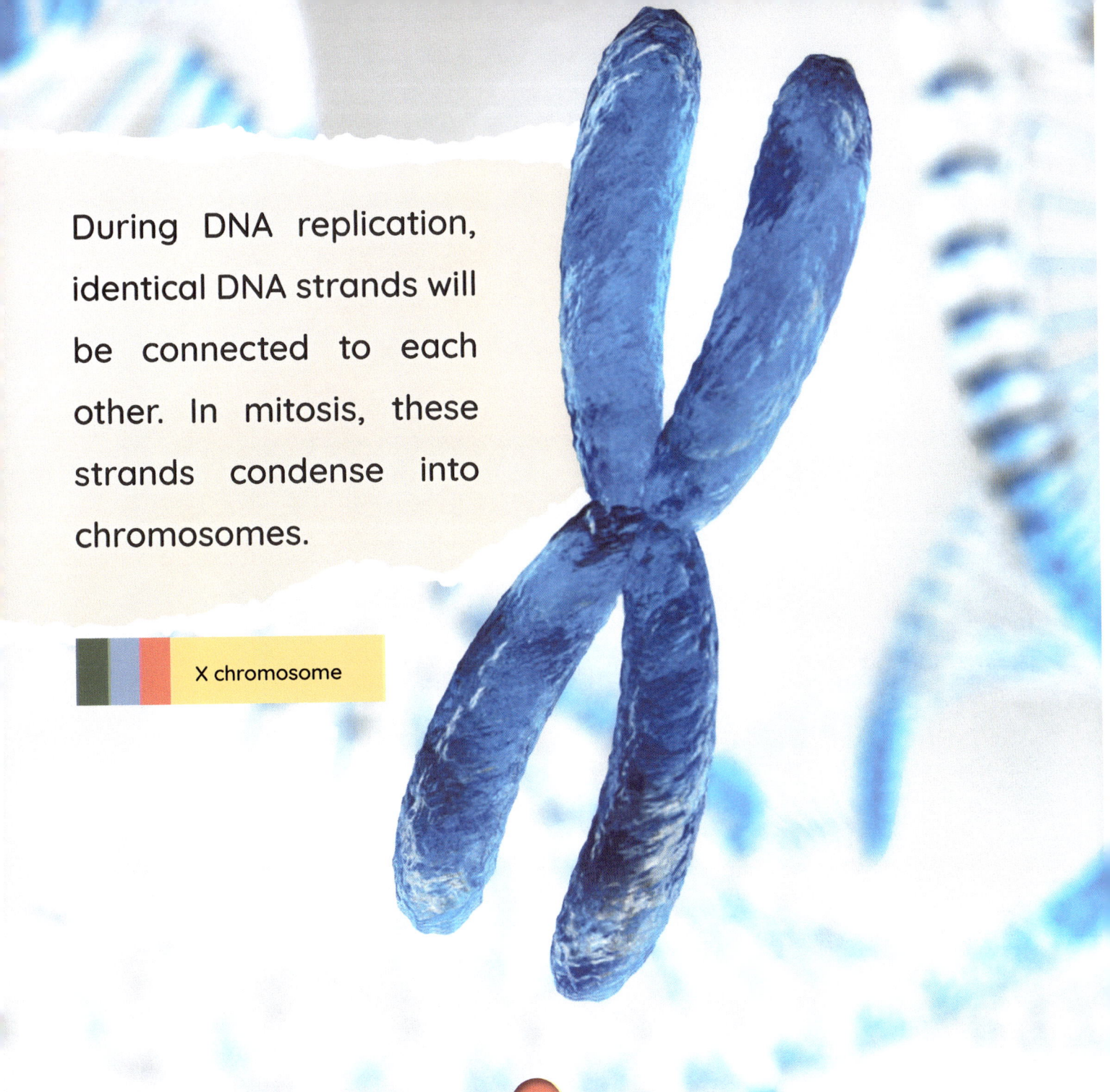

During DNA replication, identical DNA strands will be connected to each other. In mitosis, these strands condense into chromosomes.

X chromosome

MITOSIS

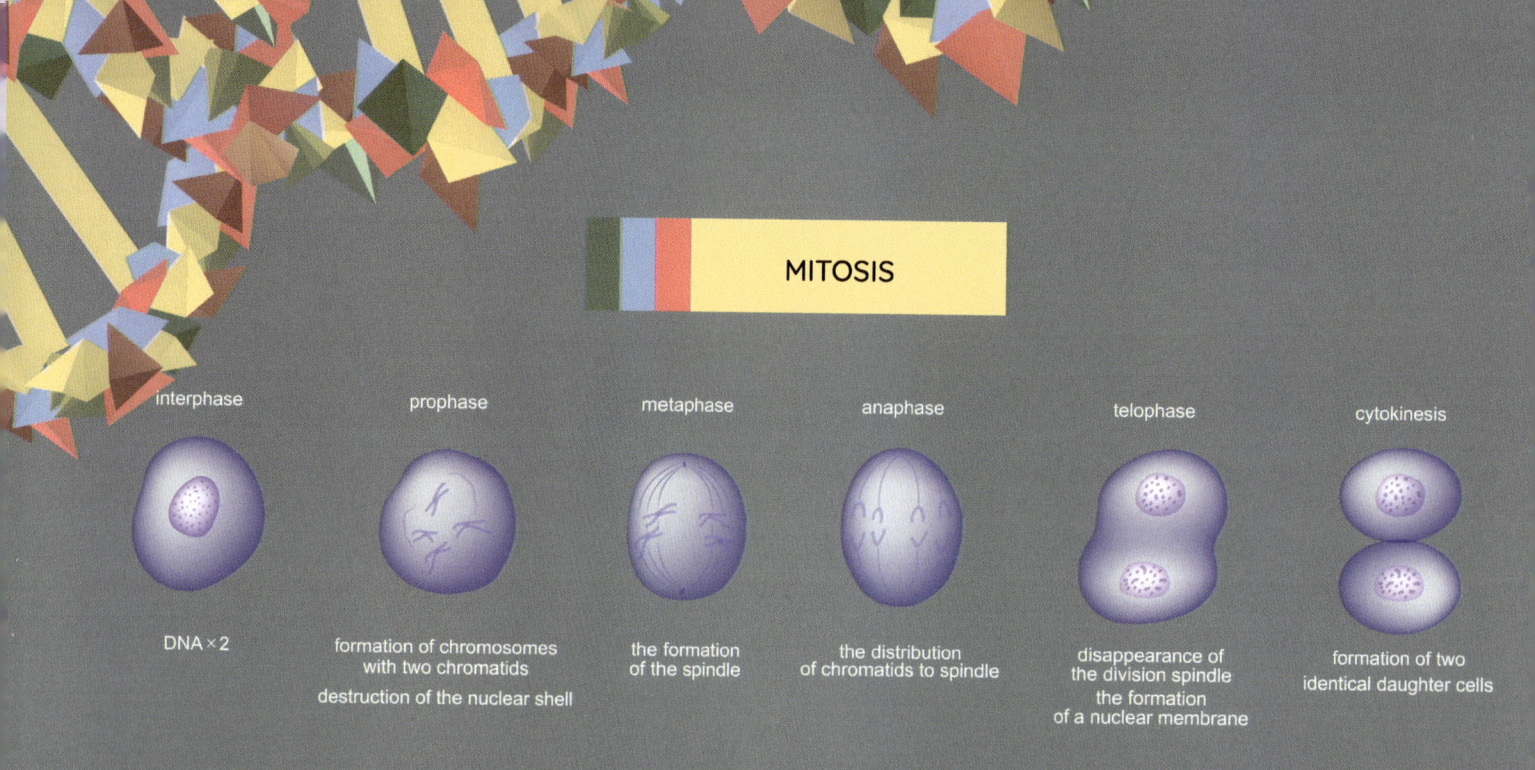

interphase	prophase	metaphase	anaphase	telophase	cytokinesis
DNA × 2	formation of chromosomes with two chromatids / destruction of the nuclear shell	the formation of the spindle	the distribution of chromatids to spindle	disappearance of the division spindle / the formation of a nuclear membrane	formation of two identical daughter cells

They are moved to the middle of the cell before finally being pulled apart. Half of the DNA goes to one side. The other half goes to the opposite side. These movements are achieved with spindle fibers. The result is identical sets of DNA going to the two daughter cells.

These daughter cells form when the parent cell divides down the middle. These daughter cells will be genetically identical to each other and the parent cell. Nonetheless, since cells in multicellular organisms specialize, this does not mean that all cells in an organism are identical in every respect.

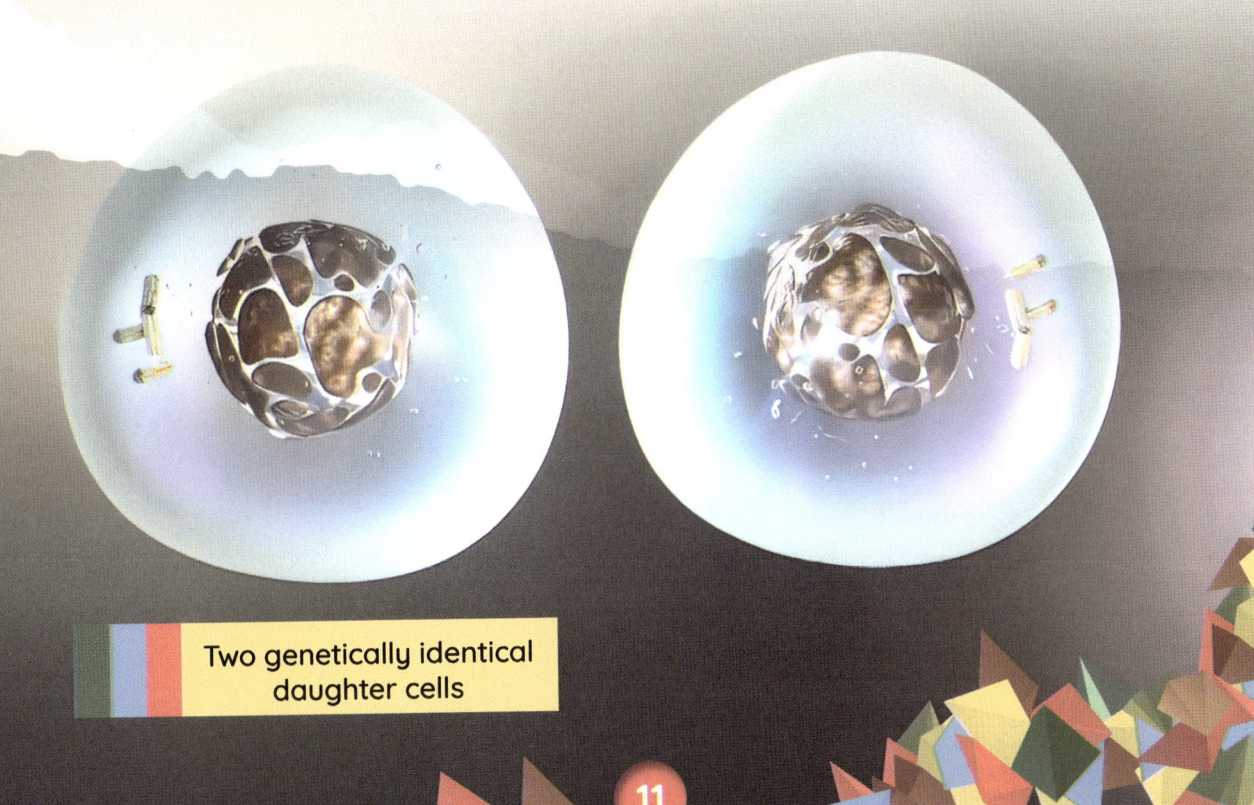

Two genetically identical daughter cells

Somatic Cells and Gametes

Multicellular organisms can have two different kinds of cells. These are somatic cells and gametes. Somatic cells are body cells. Gametes are cells used for reproduction. They are also called sex cells.

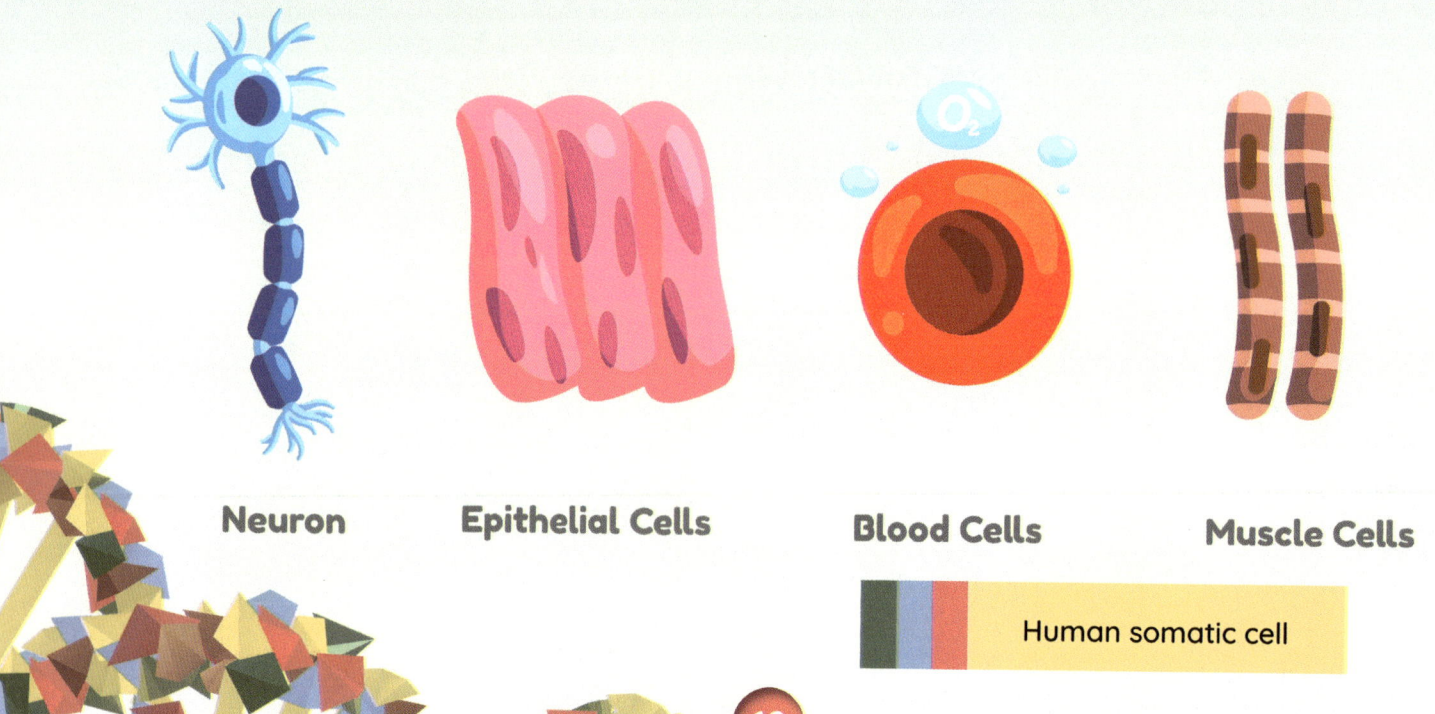

Neuron   Epithelial Cells   Blood Cells   Muscle Cells

Human somatic cell

A 3d illustration of sperm and egg cell

They result in a new organism if they fuse with another sex cell. The male sex cells are sperm cells. The female sex cells are egg cells. Sperm cells are significantly smaller than egg cells. These need to combine to create a new person.

DNA replication

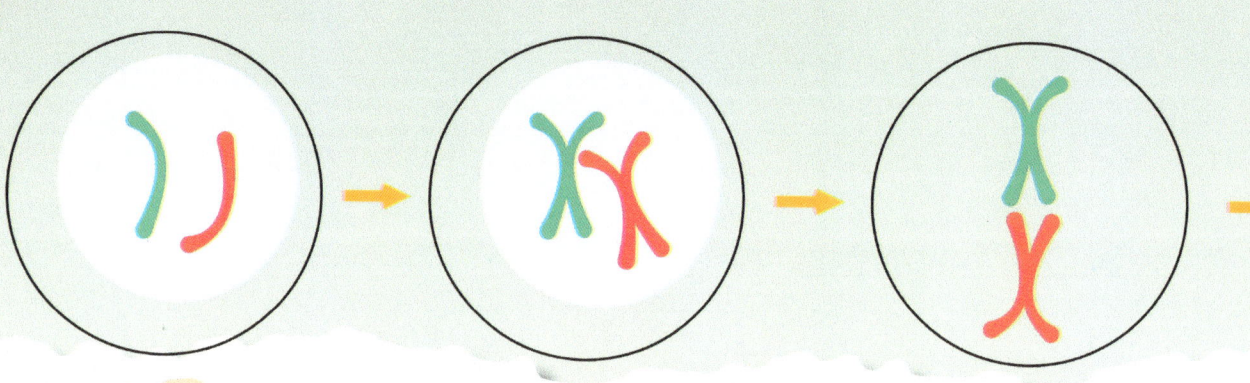

Most cells in the body are somatic cells. These cells are diploid. This means they contain pairs of chromosomes. Humans have 23 pairs for a total of 46 chromosomes. One pair comes from your father. The other pair is from your mother. Somatic cells form through mitosis.

Mitosis

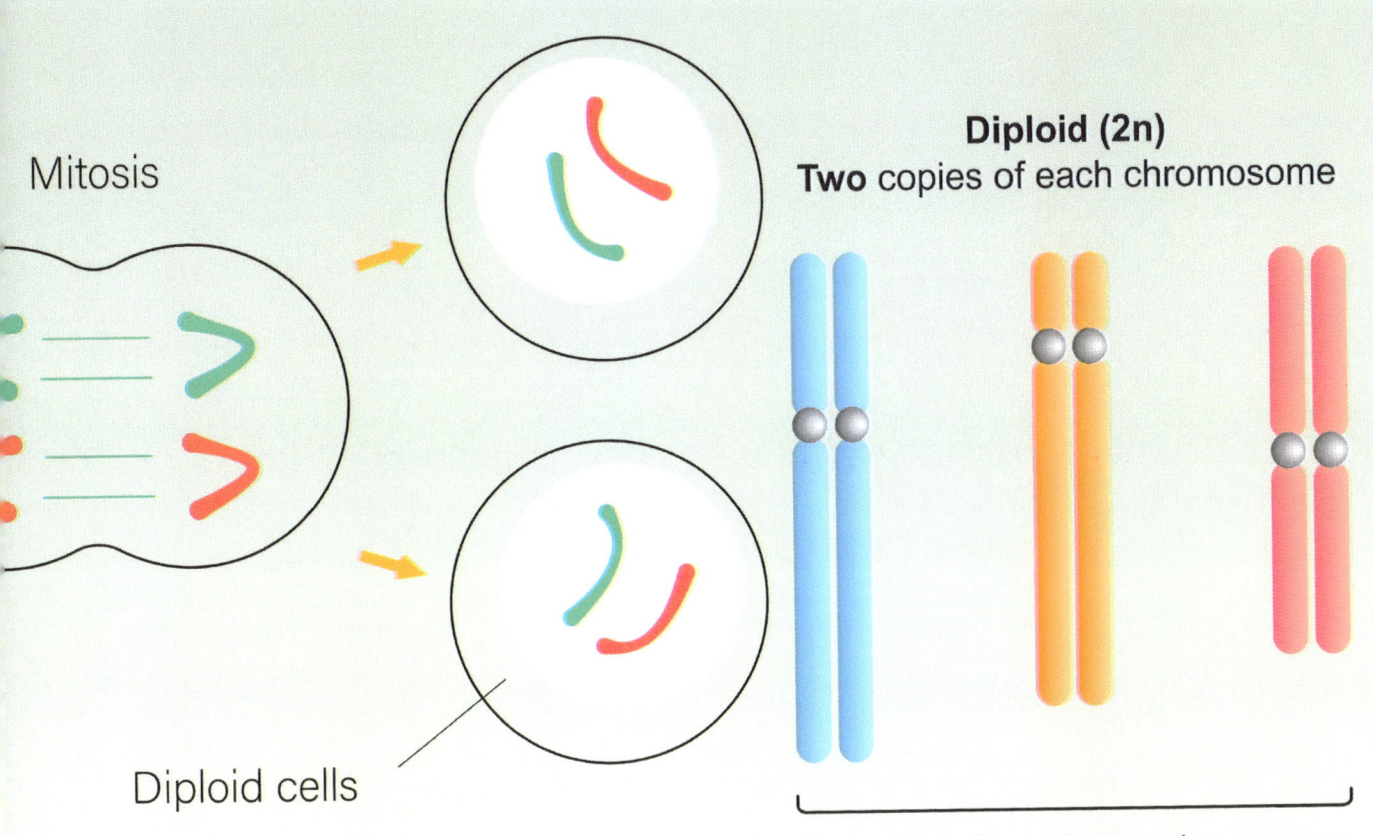

Diploid cells

Diploid (2n)
Two copies of each chromosome

Three pairs of homologous chromosomes
(of maternal and paternal origin)

Diploid animal cells

Gametes or sex cells are haploid cells. This means they only have half the number of chromosomes. They are unpaired. This means that human gametes will only have 23 chromosomes. This is fortunate because when they fuse with a gamete from the opposite sex, (male sex cells fuse with female sex cells), the result will have 46 chromosomes. This is a new, genetically unique, individual!

Haploid (n)

- Refer to one set of chromosome (n)
- In human, (n) = 23 chromosomes
- Only gametes (sperm & ova) are haploid

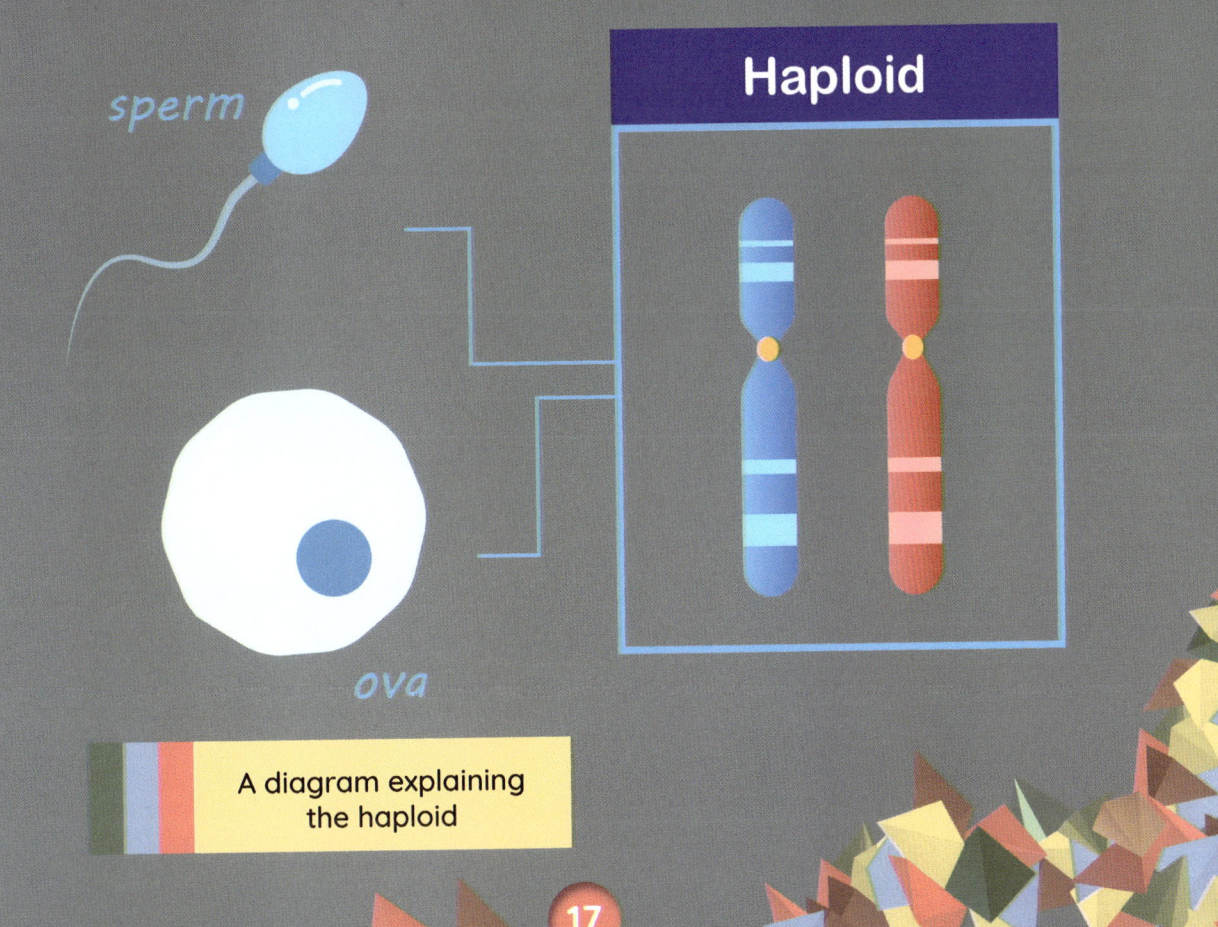

sperm

ova

Haploid

A diagram explaining the haploid

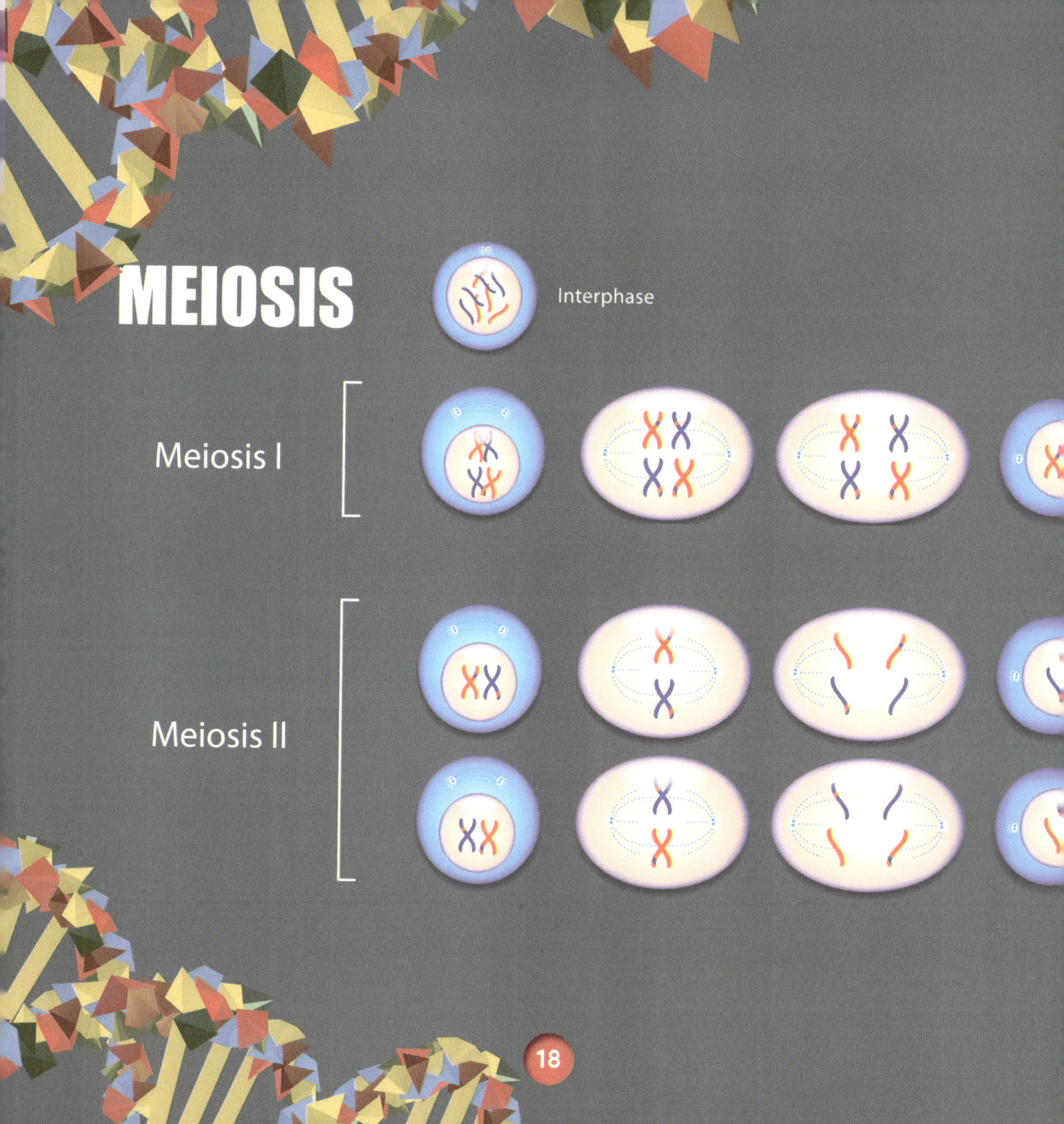

MEIOSIS

Interphase

Meiosis I

Meiosis II

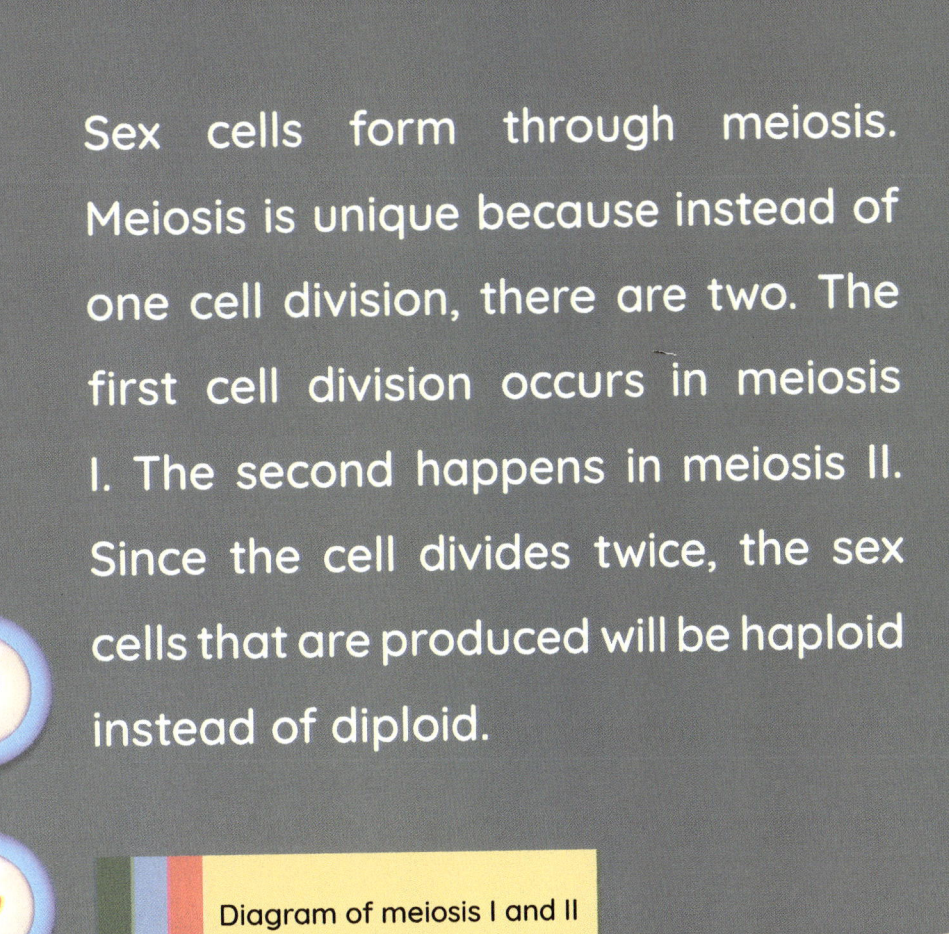

Sex cells form through meiosis. Meiosis is unique because instead of one cell division, there are two. The first cell division occurs in meiosis I. The second happens in meiosis II. Since the cell divides twice, the sex cells that are produced will be haploid instead of diploid.

Diagram of meiosis I and II

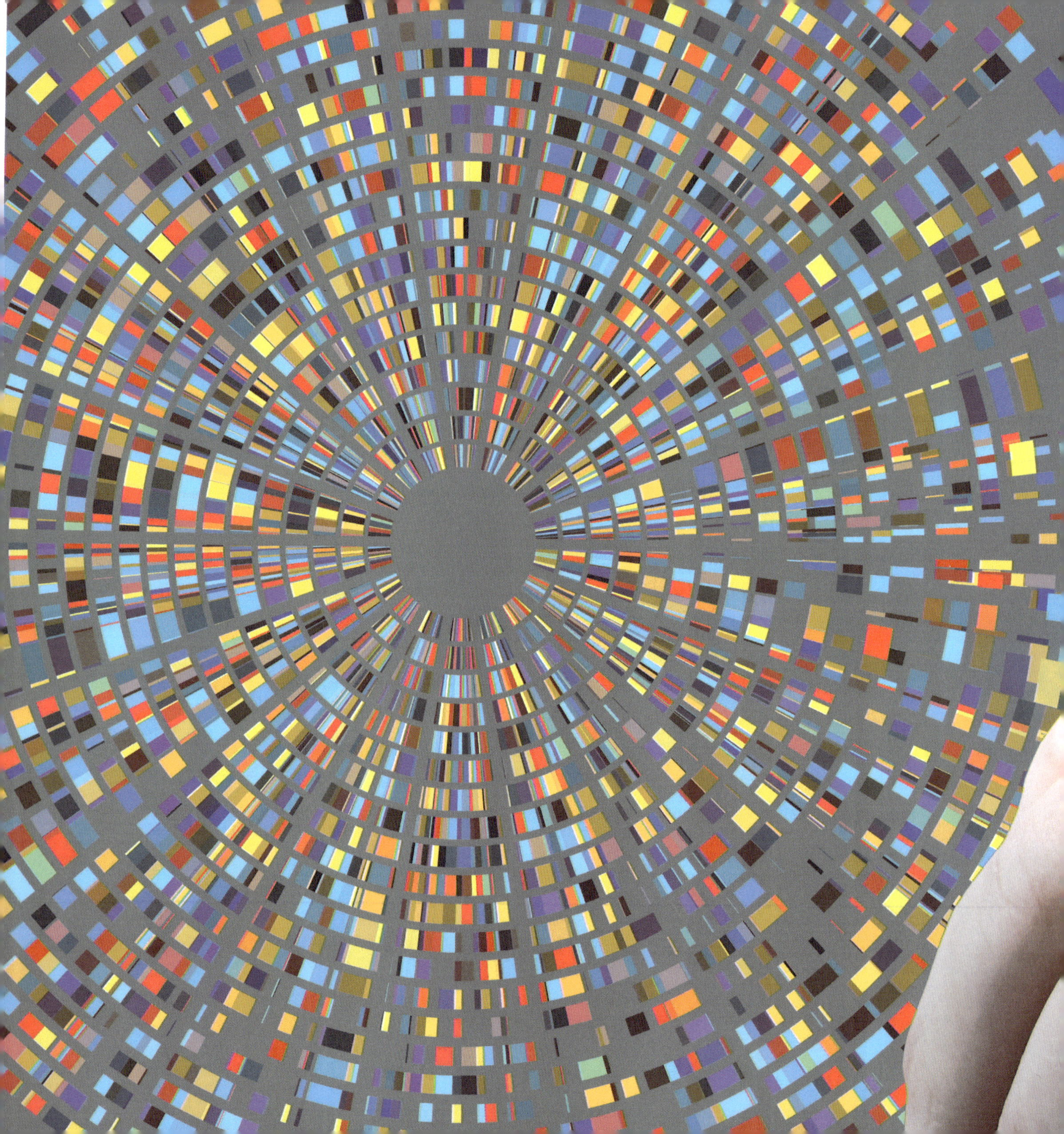

CHAPTER 2
The Stages of Meiosis

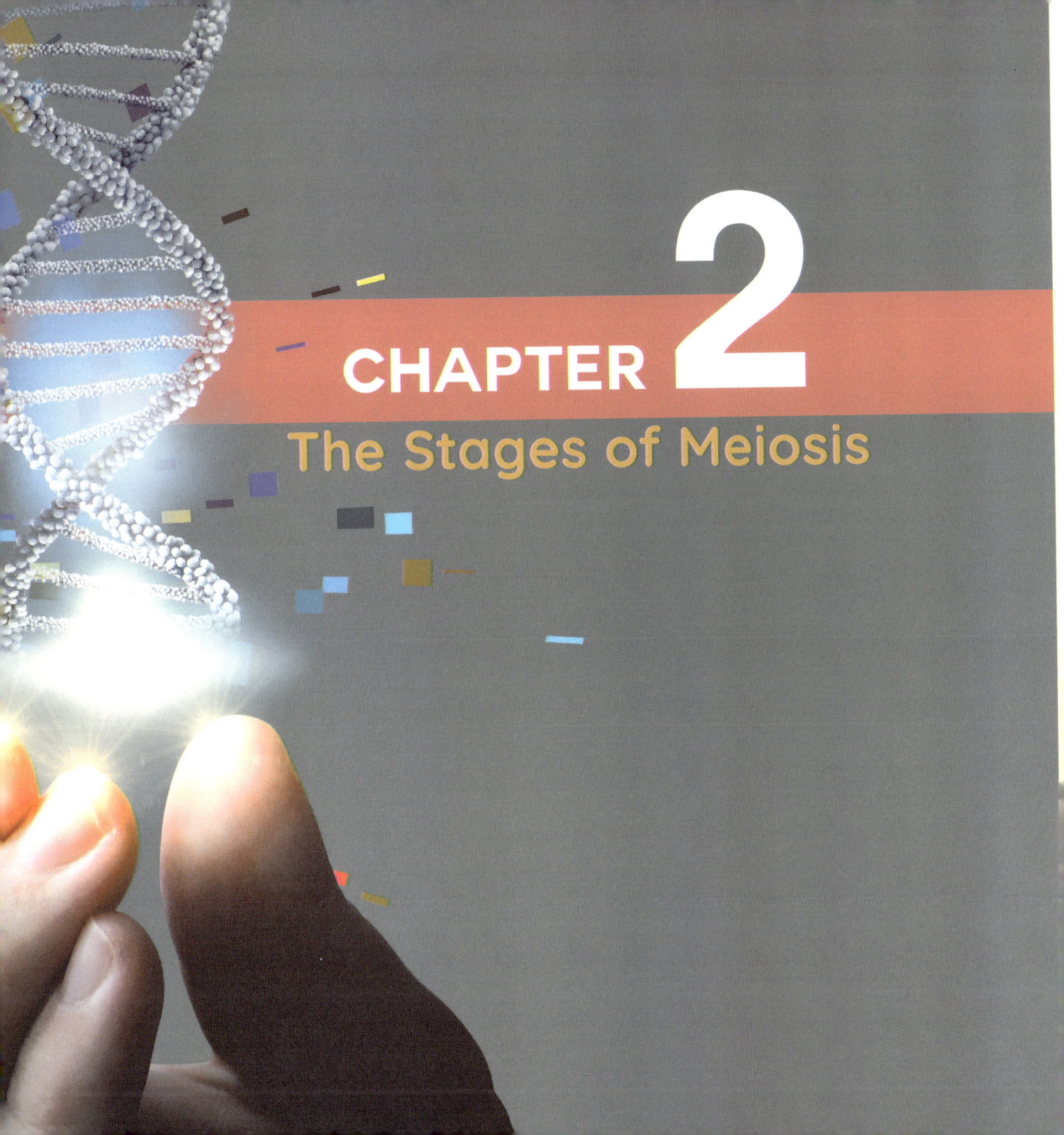

Meiosis is broken into two stages. Each stage is made up of the same four steps. These are prophase, metaphase, anaphase, and telophase. The stage they belong to is marked with Roman numerals. For example, if prophase happens in the first stage of meiosis, it is called prophase I.

Meosis has two stages and each stage has the same four steps.

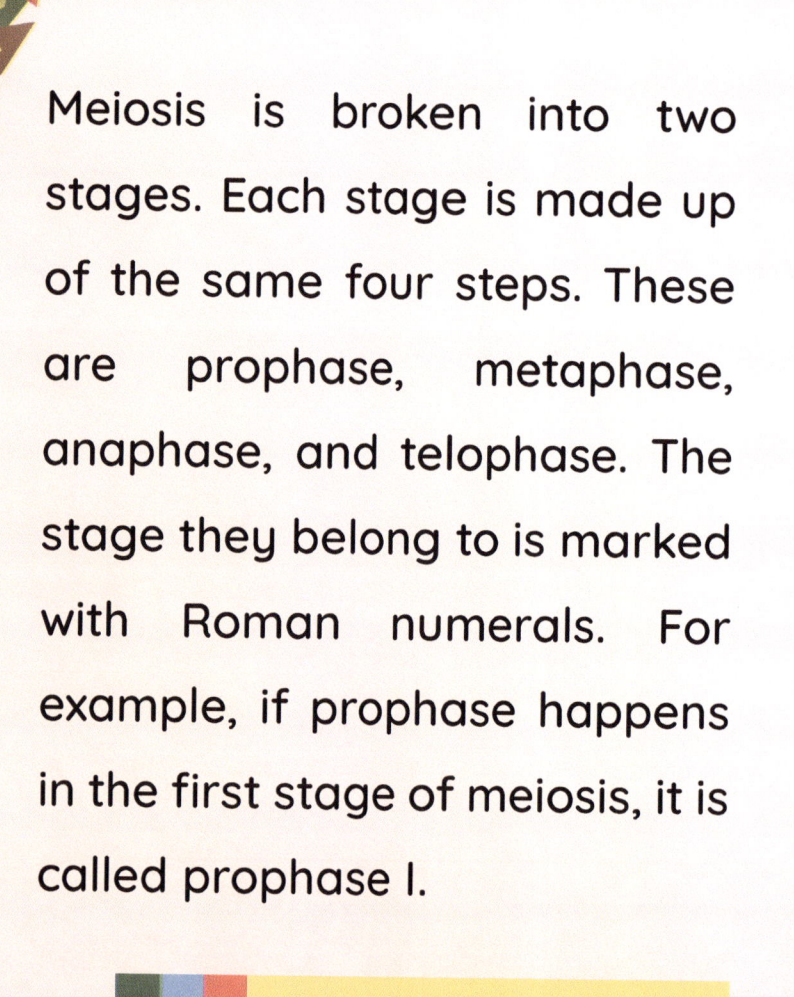

Prophase I

Prophase II

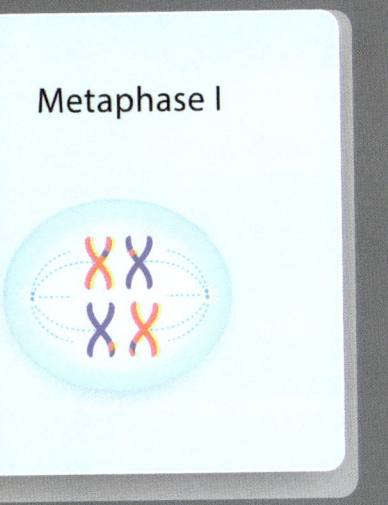

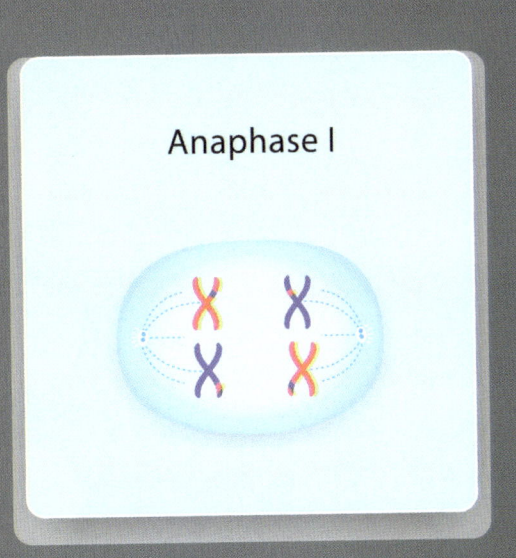

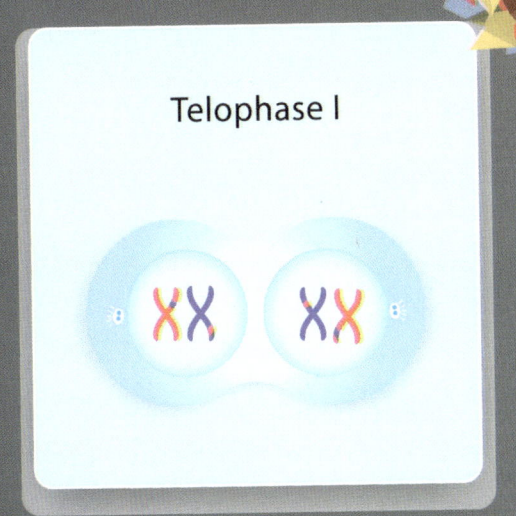

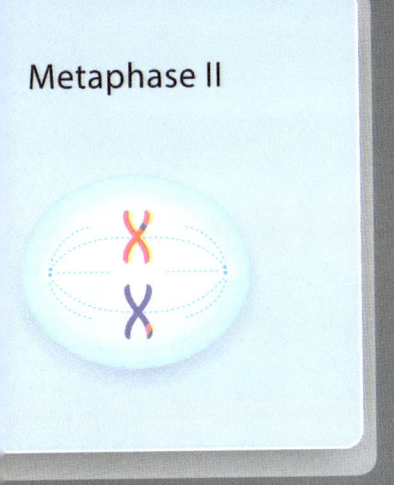

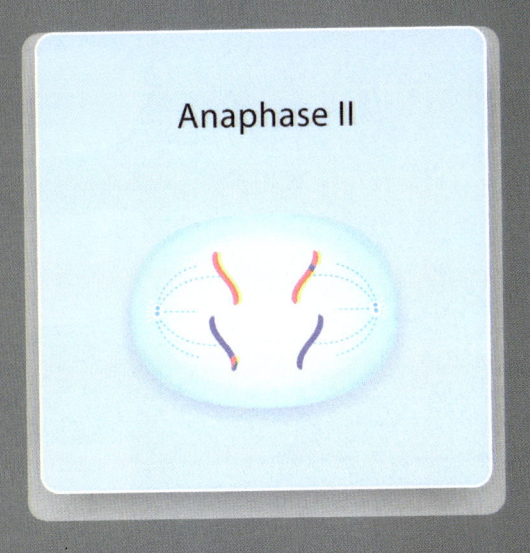

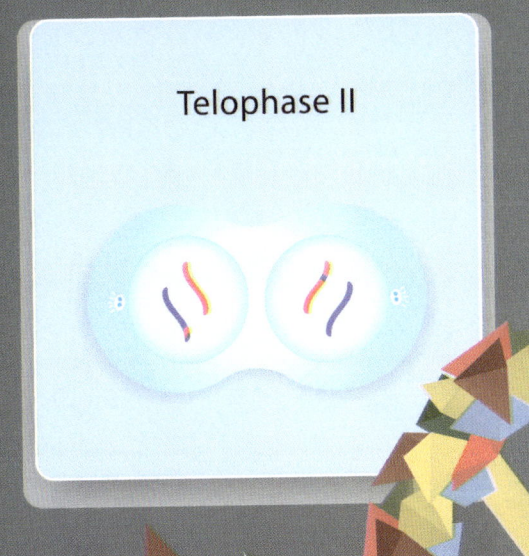

Metaphase I	Anaphase I	Telophase I
Metaphase II	Anaphase II	Telophase II

Stage One: PROPHASE I

During this part of meiosis, the DNA will condense into chromosomes. Each chromosome will consist of two rod-like structures. These structures are identical genetically. Each individual rod is called a chromatin and the identical pairs are called sister chromatids.

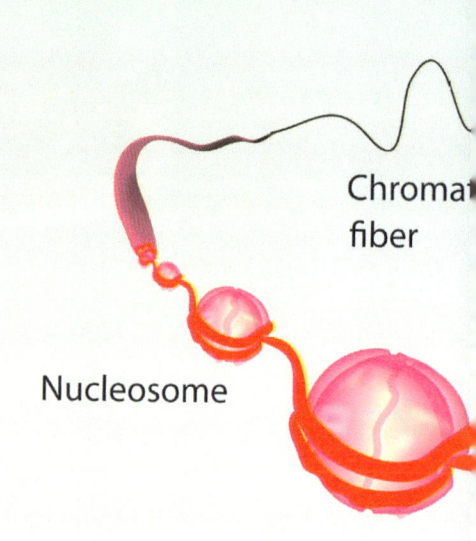

Chromosome

Chromatin fiber

Nucleosome

Prophase

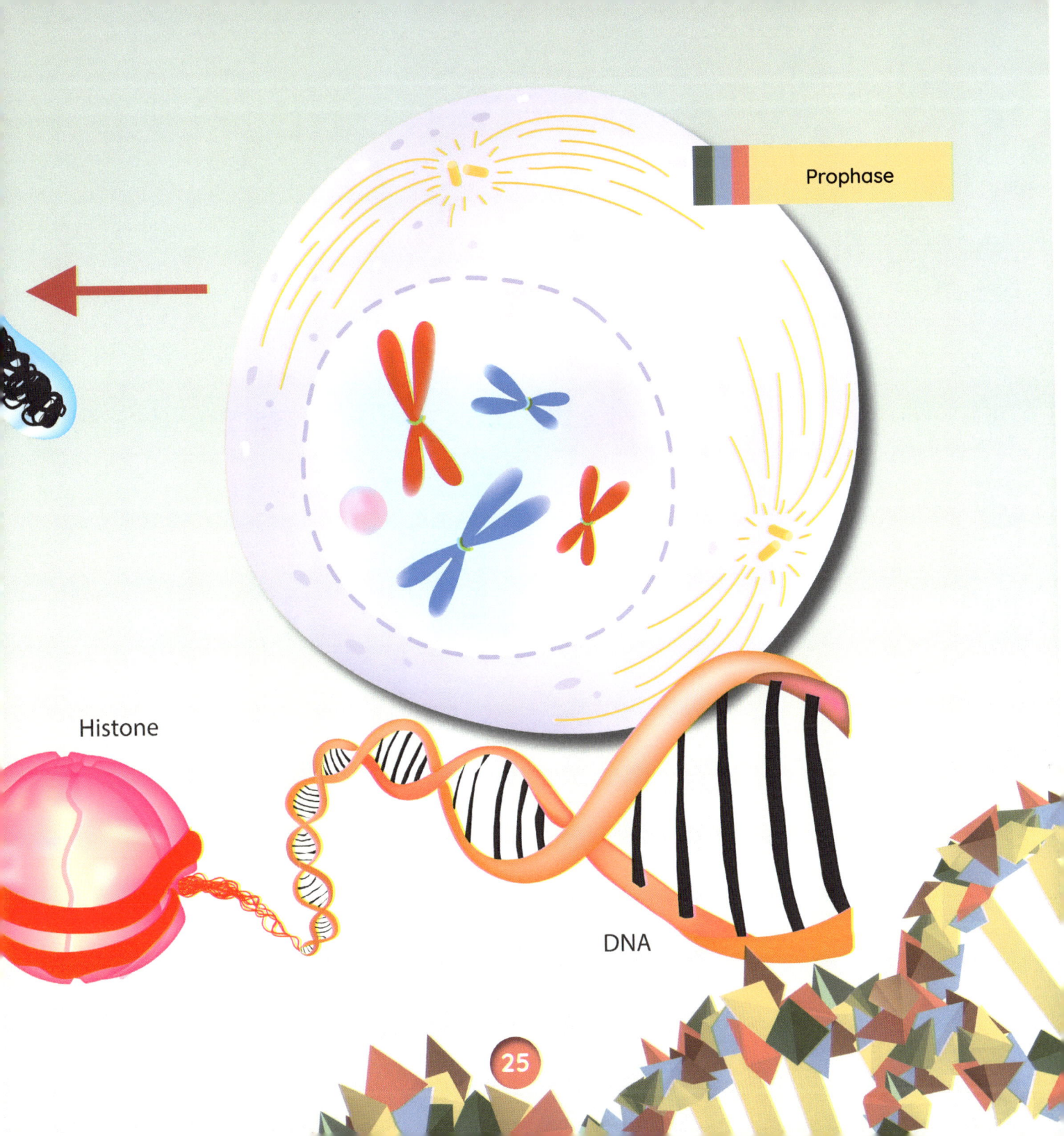

Histone

DNA

Each chromosome will line up to pair with their mate. When this happens, the chromosomes will exchange genetic material. This is called crossing over. This process can result in new combinations of alleles. Alleles are variations of the same gene.

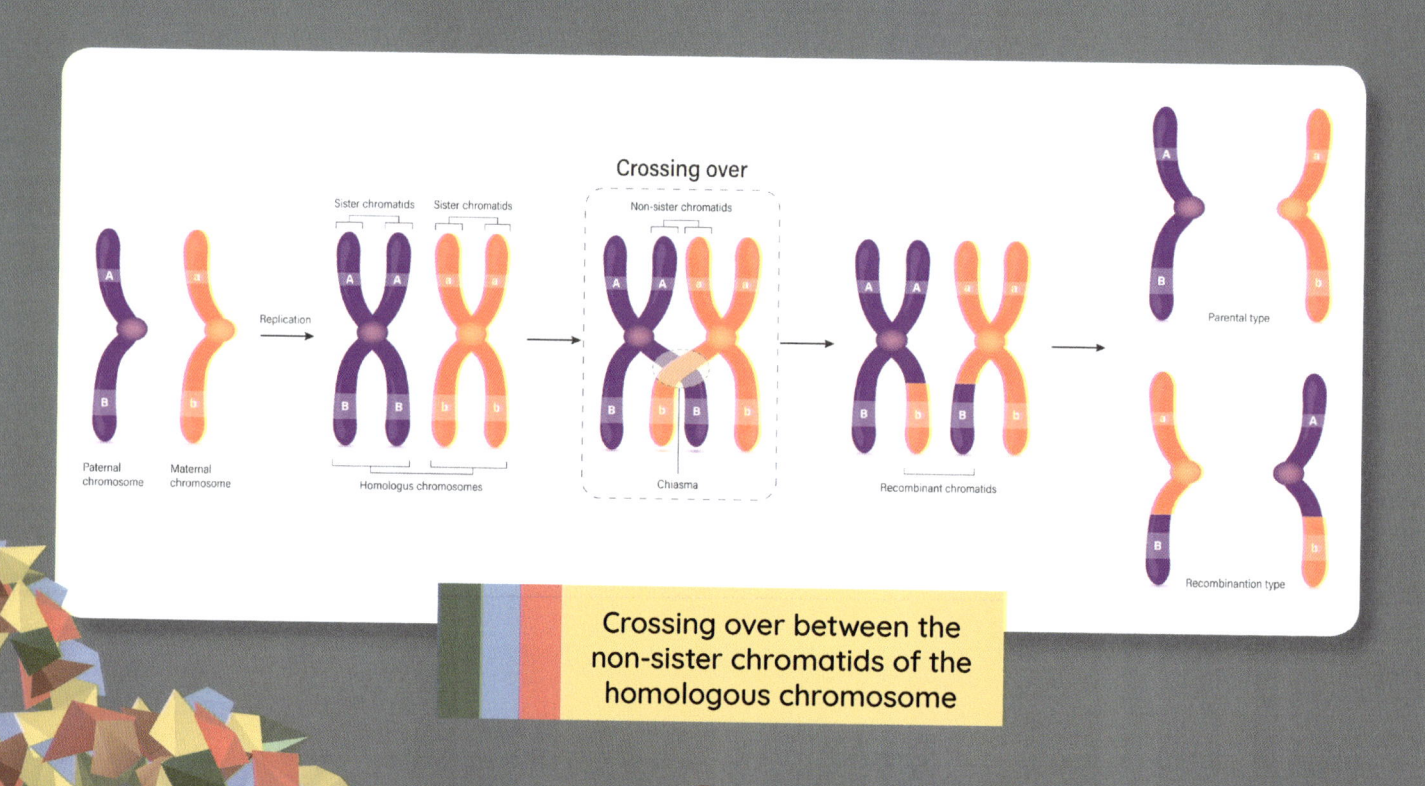

Crossing over between the non-sister chromatids of the homologous chromosome

Spindle   Chiasma

Sister chromatids

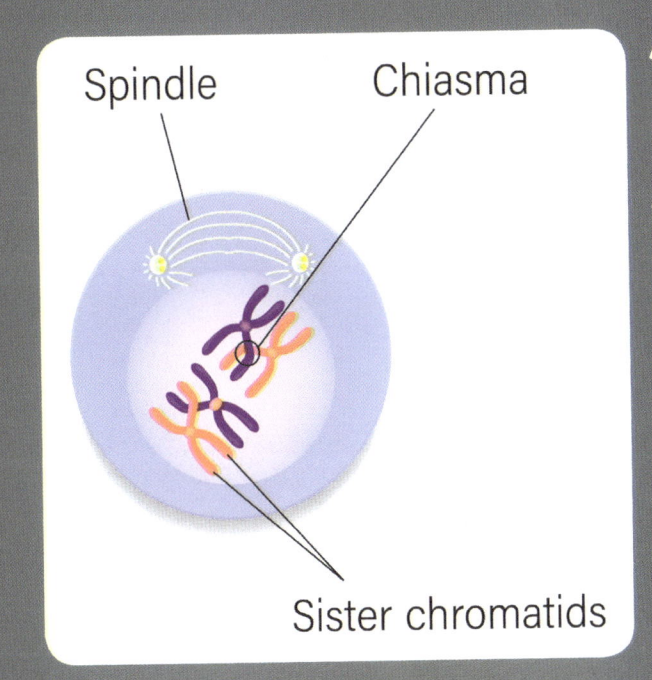

Spindle fiber forming in prophase stage

As the chromosomes pair up, the nuclear membrane that protects them will begin to dissolve. The spindle fibers also begin to form. These will later grasp onto the chromosomes to pull them to opposite sides of the cell. This is possible since the nuclear membrane has dissolved. Prophase I is the longest step of meiosis.

Metaphase I

Metaphase I is when the chromosome pairs will line up along the middle of the cell. This is sometimes called the equator. The spindle fibers will be attached to the chromosomes to move them around.

Metaphase, the second stage of meiosis.

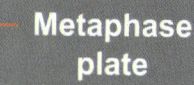

Anaphase I

Anaphase I is when chromosomes separate. One half of the pair will go to one side of the cell. The other half will go to the opposite side of the cell. This results in identical DNA on opposite sides.

Sister chromatids

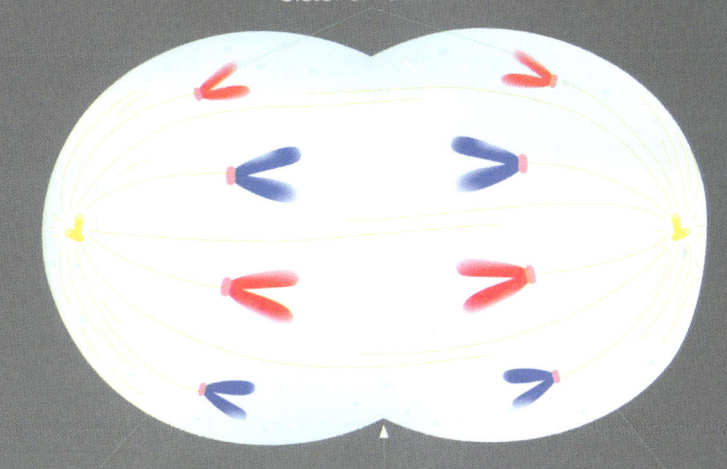

Plasma membrane Cleavage furrow Cytosol
(Cytokinesis)

Anaphase

Telophase I

This is the last stage of meiosis I. This is the step where nuclear membranes will reform around the chromosomes. The cytoplasm will also begin to pinch and divide. Finally, during cytokinesis, the cell will split into two.

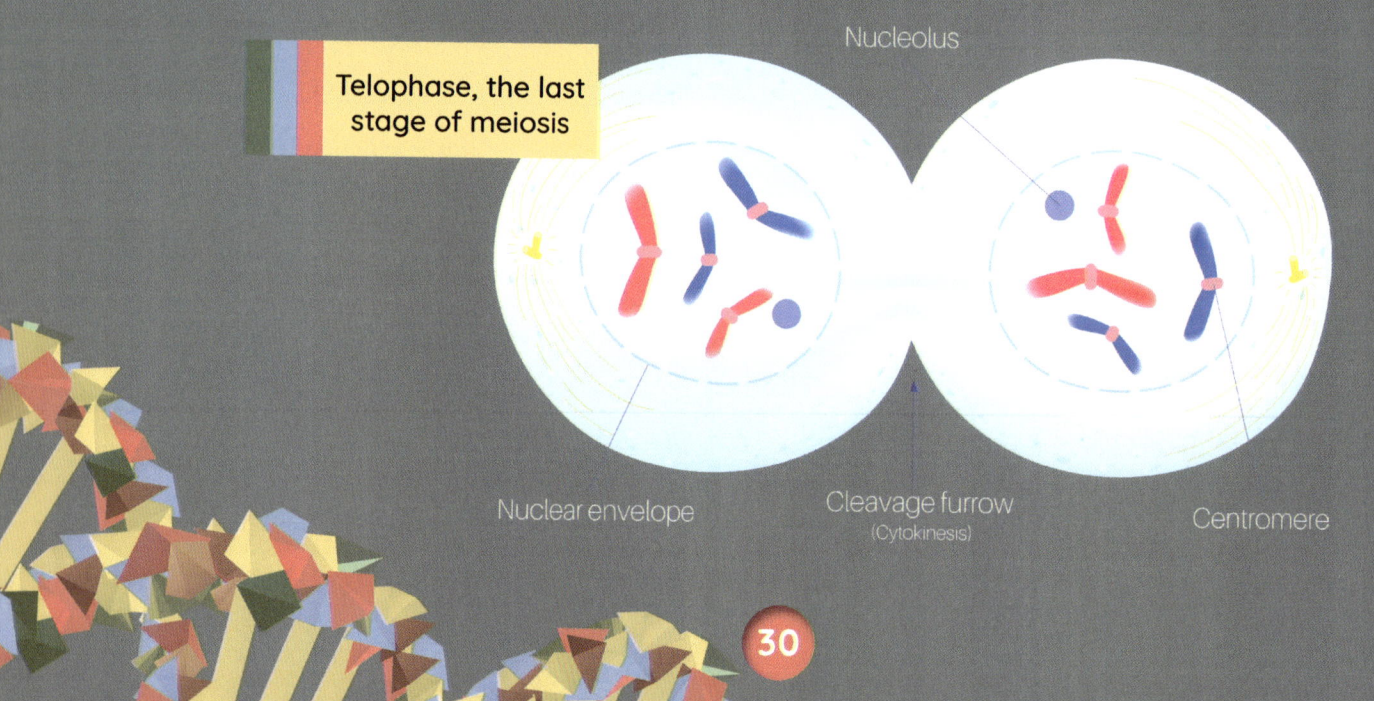

Telophase, the last stage of meiosis

Nucleolus

Nuclear envelope

Cleavage furrow
(Cytokinesis)

Centromere

Sometimes, the reformation of the nuclear membranes will not happen. This is because the process of meiosis is not yet finished. The result of stage one of meiosis are two haploid daughter cells.

Two daughter cells

Stage Two

In many respects, stage two can be thought of as being mitosis except that it results in haploid cells.

Prophase II

The two daughter cells formed during meiosis I will both head straight into meiosis II. Once again, the DNA will condense into chromosomes. These are made up of two identical rods. Spindle fibers will also form once again and the nuclear membrane will disappear if it has been reformed.

PROPHASE II

In prophase II, the DNA will again condense into chromosomes

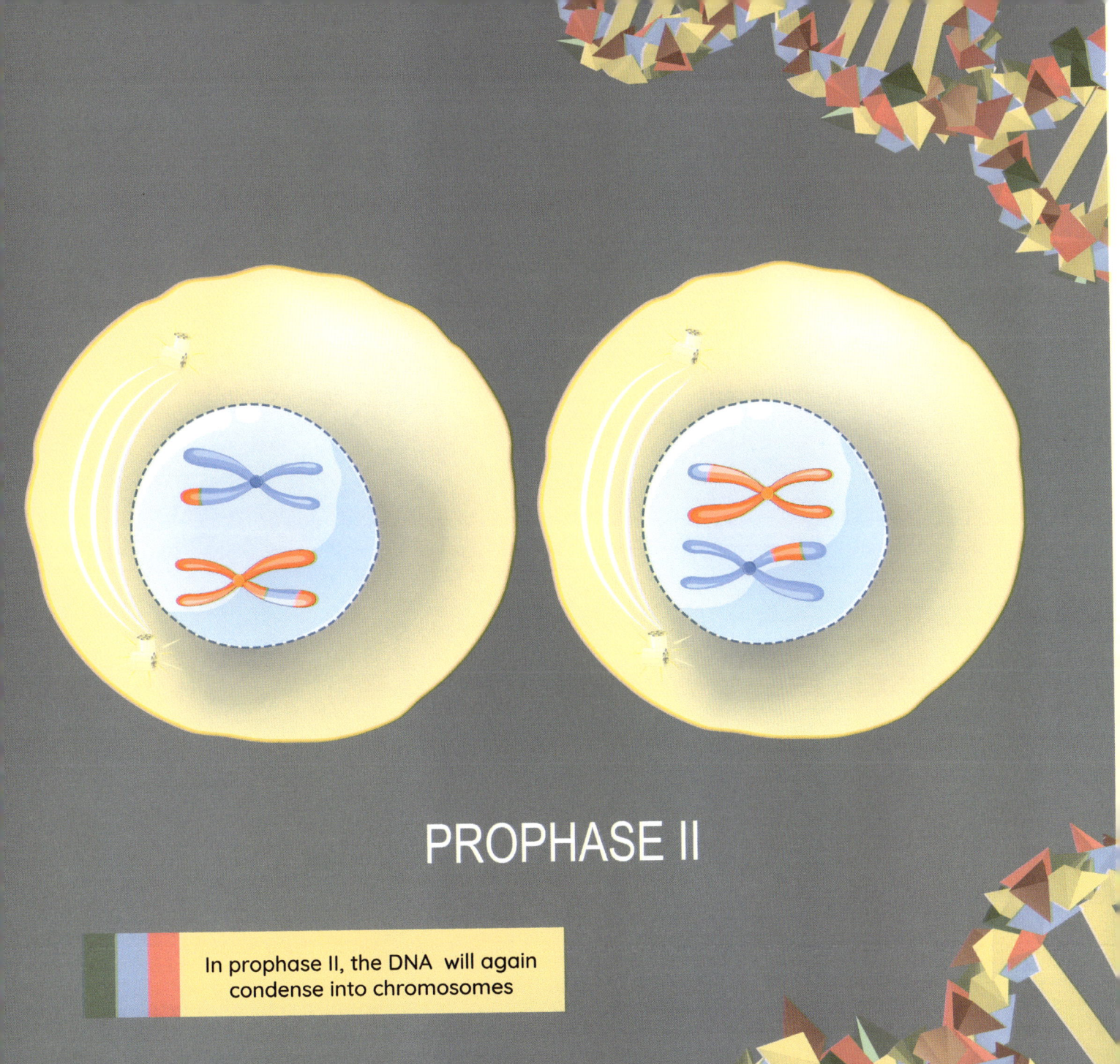

Metaphase II

During metaphase II, chromosomes will line up along the middle of the cell. Spindle fibers will attach to both the chromosomes.

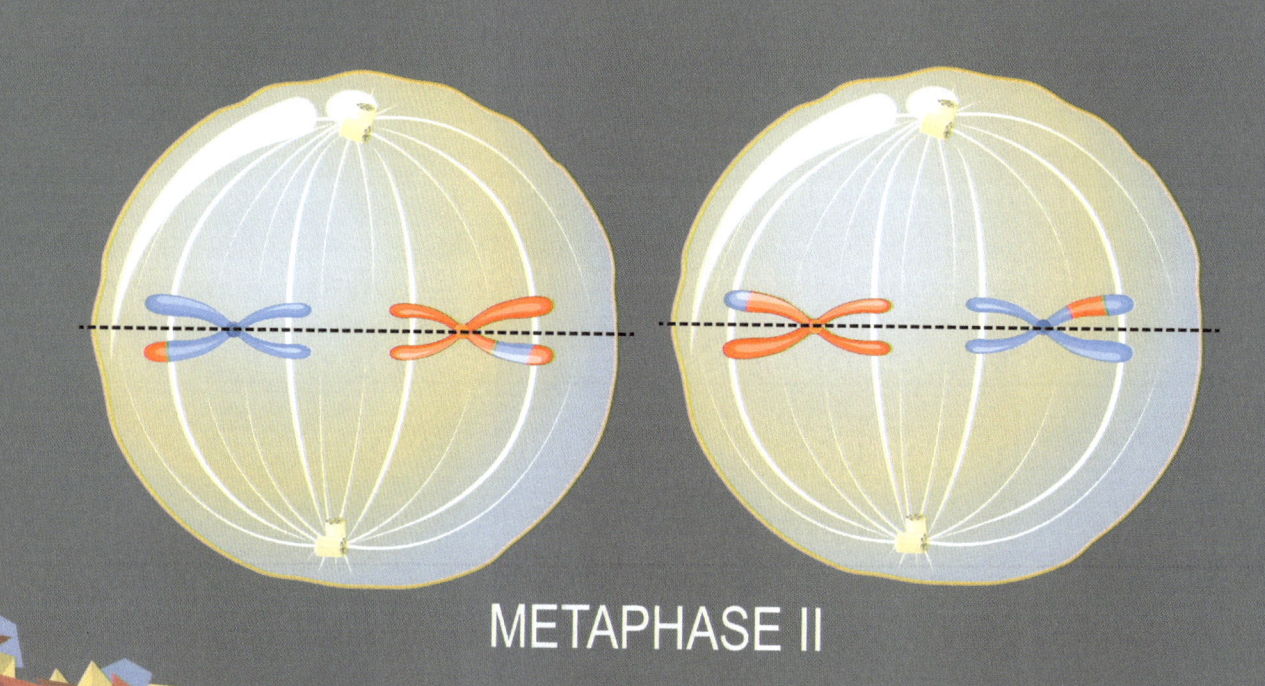

METAPHASE II

Anaphase II

During this phase, each chromosome will be pulled apart by the spindle fibers. One rod each will go to opposite sides of the cell. These are the sister chromatids being pulled apart.

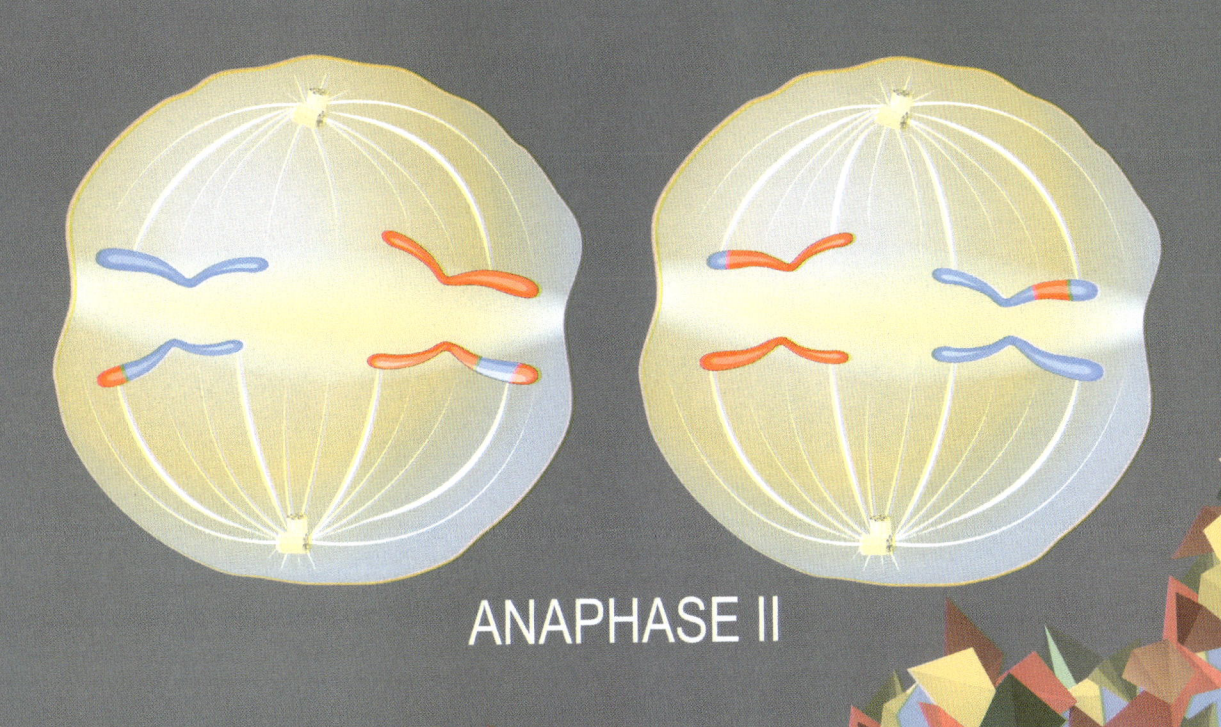

ANAPHASE II

Telophase II

During this step the spindle fibers will disappear. The nuclear membrane will reform around the chromosomes. The cytoplasm will begin to divide. Finally, cytokinesis will happen. The result is four haploid cells.

These cells are sex cells because each one has half the number of cells than the parent cell had before meiosis began. These haploid cells are also genetically distinct.

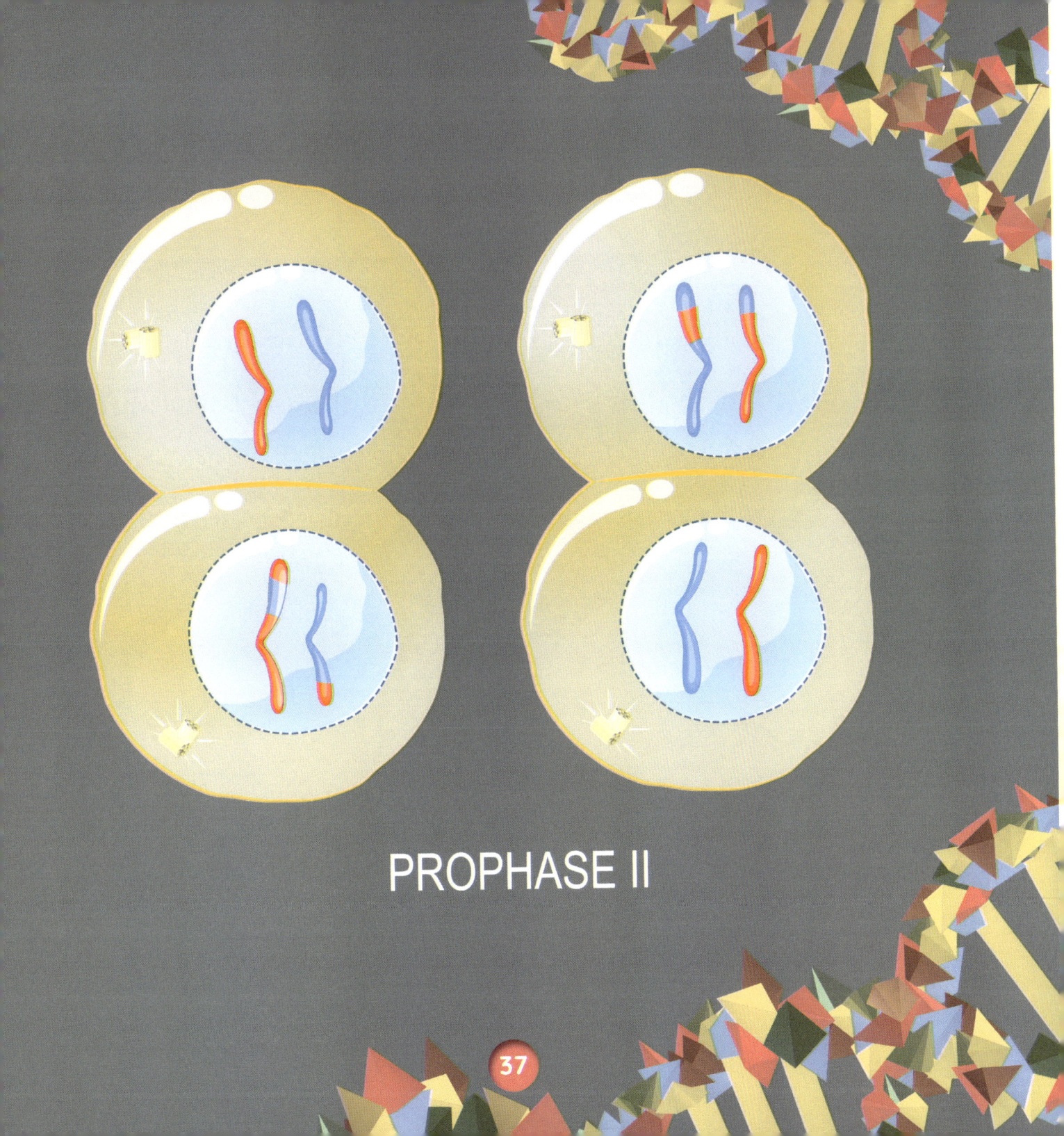

PROPHASE II

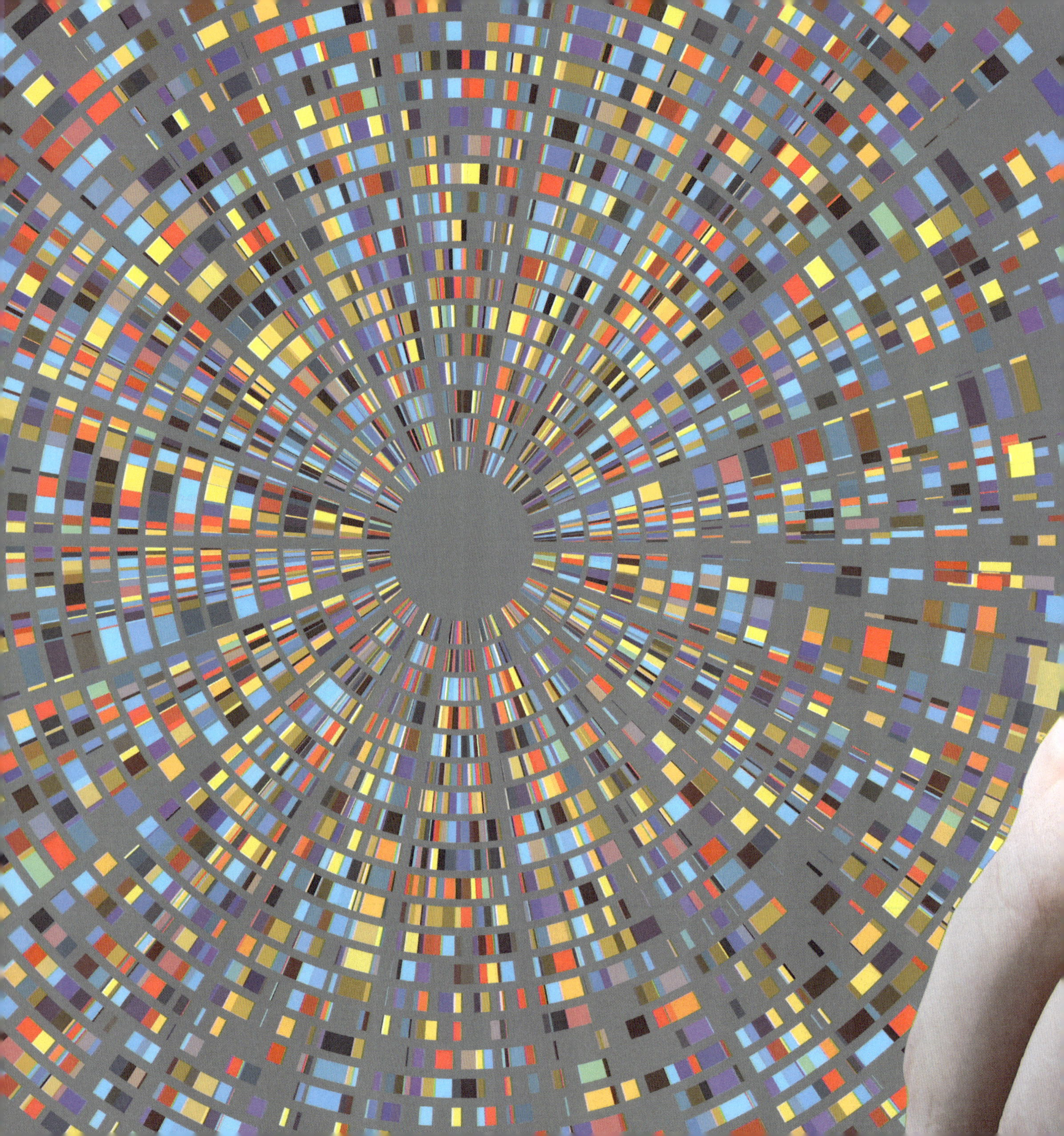

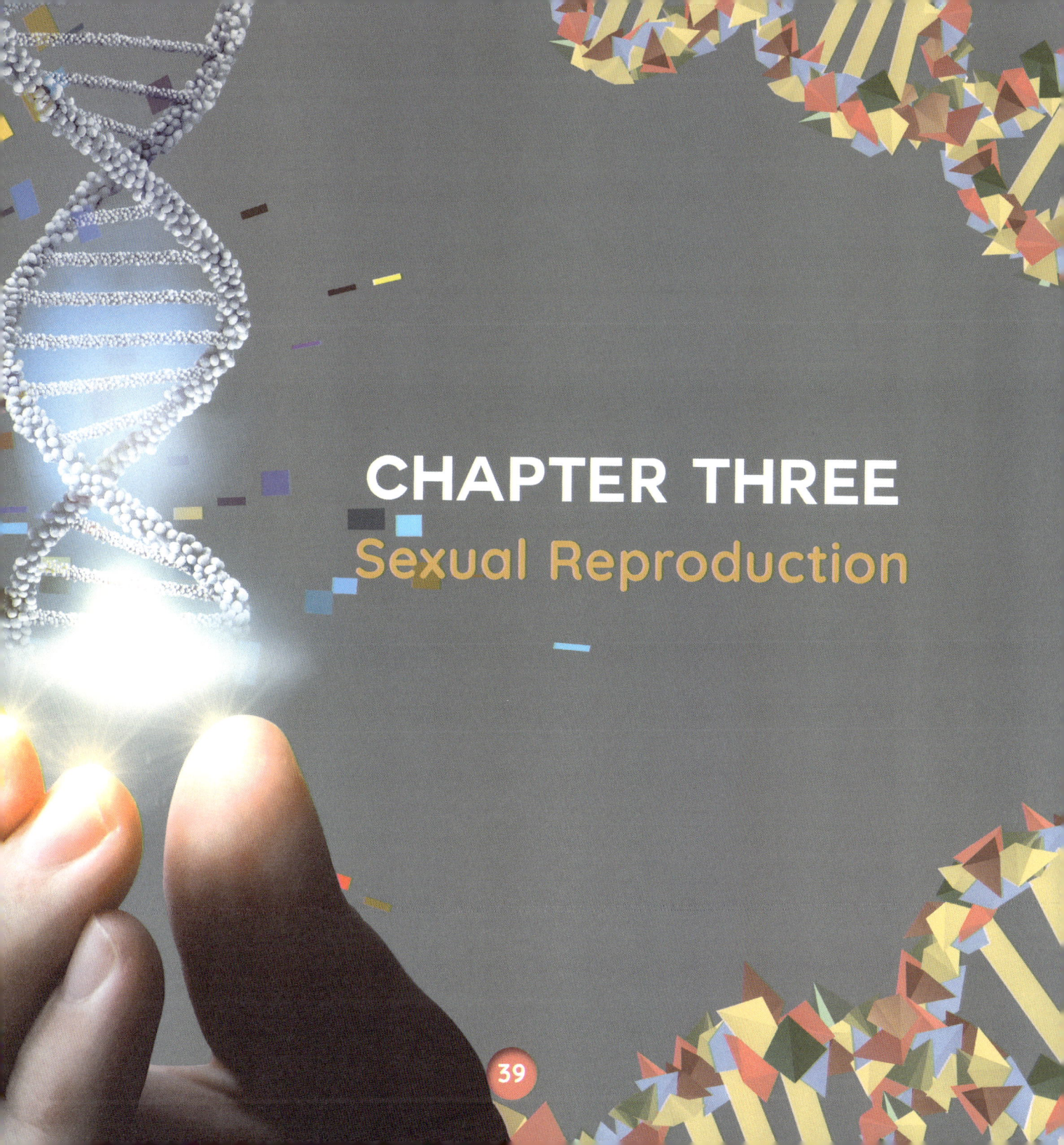

CHAPTER THREE
Sexual Reproduction

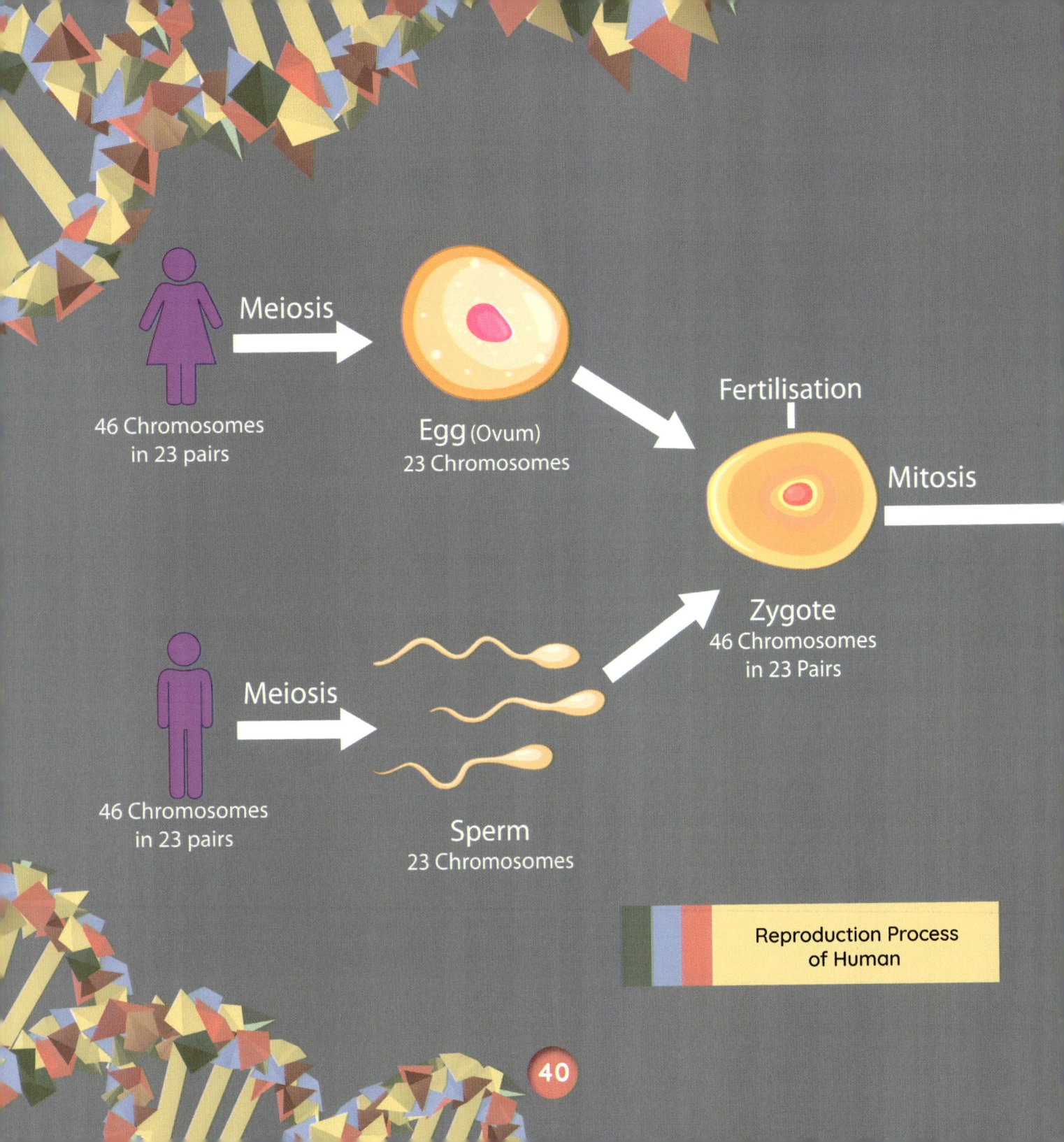

Meiosis

46 Chromosomes in 23 pairs

Egg (Ovum) 23 Chromosomes

Fertilisation

Zygote 46 Chromosomes in 23 Pairs

Mitosis

Meiosis

46 Chromosomes in 23 pairs

Sperm 23 Chromosomes

Reproduction Process of Human

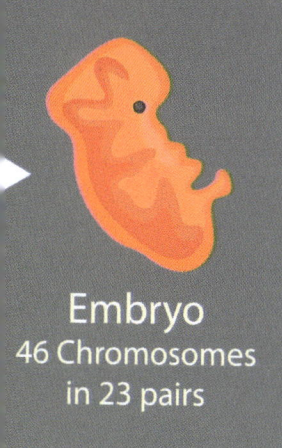

Meiosis is important because it results in cells that are haploid and genetically diverse. The cells being haploid means gametes can fuse together. Humans have 46 chromosomes. To reproduce, each sex cell needs to have 23 chromosomes. These can combine to make 46.

Embryo
46 Chromosomes in 23 pairs

We also do not want people to be genetically identical. Mixing genes from both parents helps with this, but so does the crossing over in prophase I. There is also independent assortment. This means the chromosomes line up randomly in metaphase I. This chapter will explain more about the importance of meiosis in sexual reproduction. It will explain why meiosis can offer an advantage.

MEIOSIS (Prophase I)

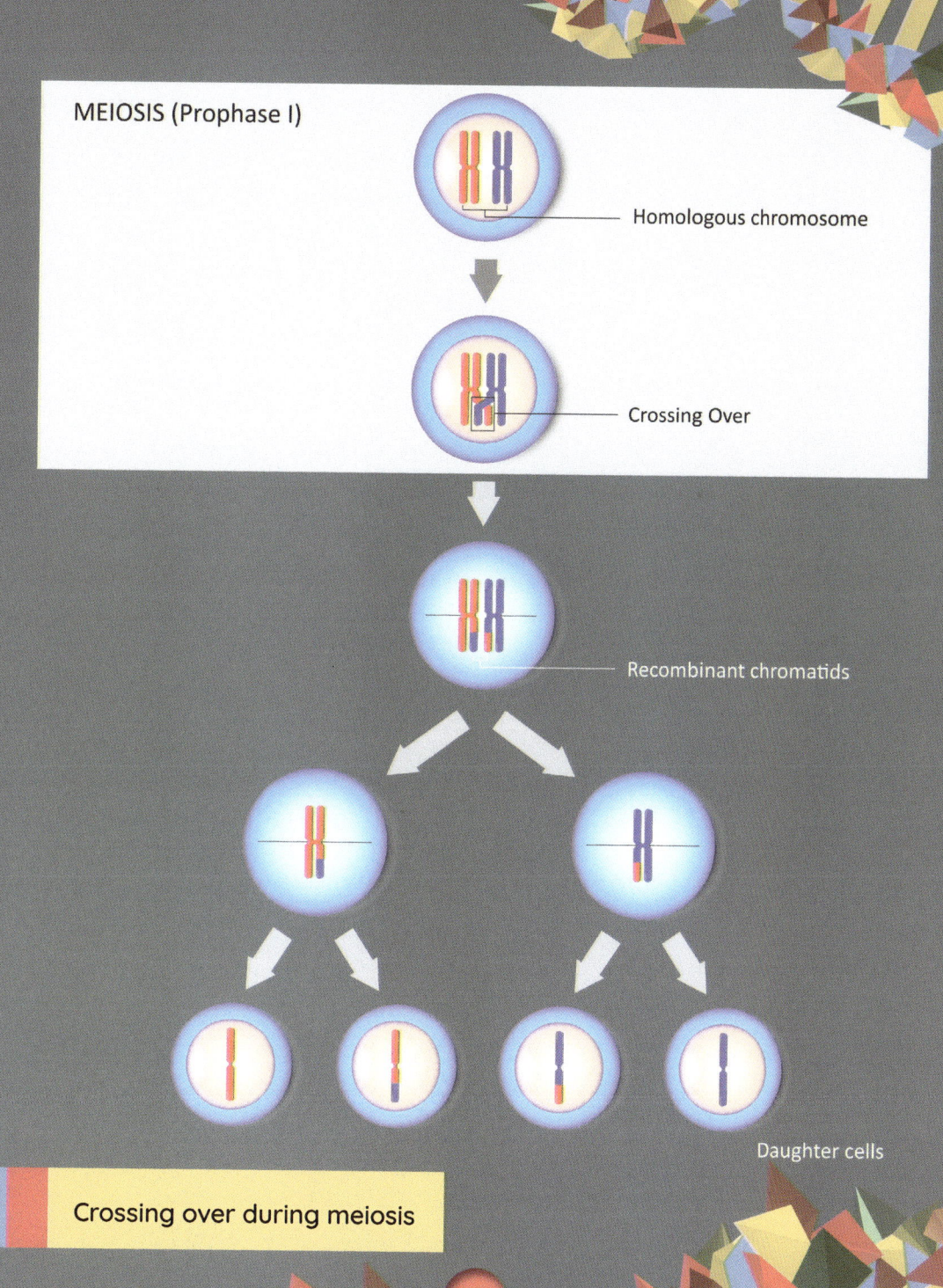

- Homologous chromosome
- Crossing Over
- Recombinant chromatids
- Daughter cells

Crossing over during meiosis

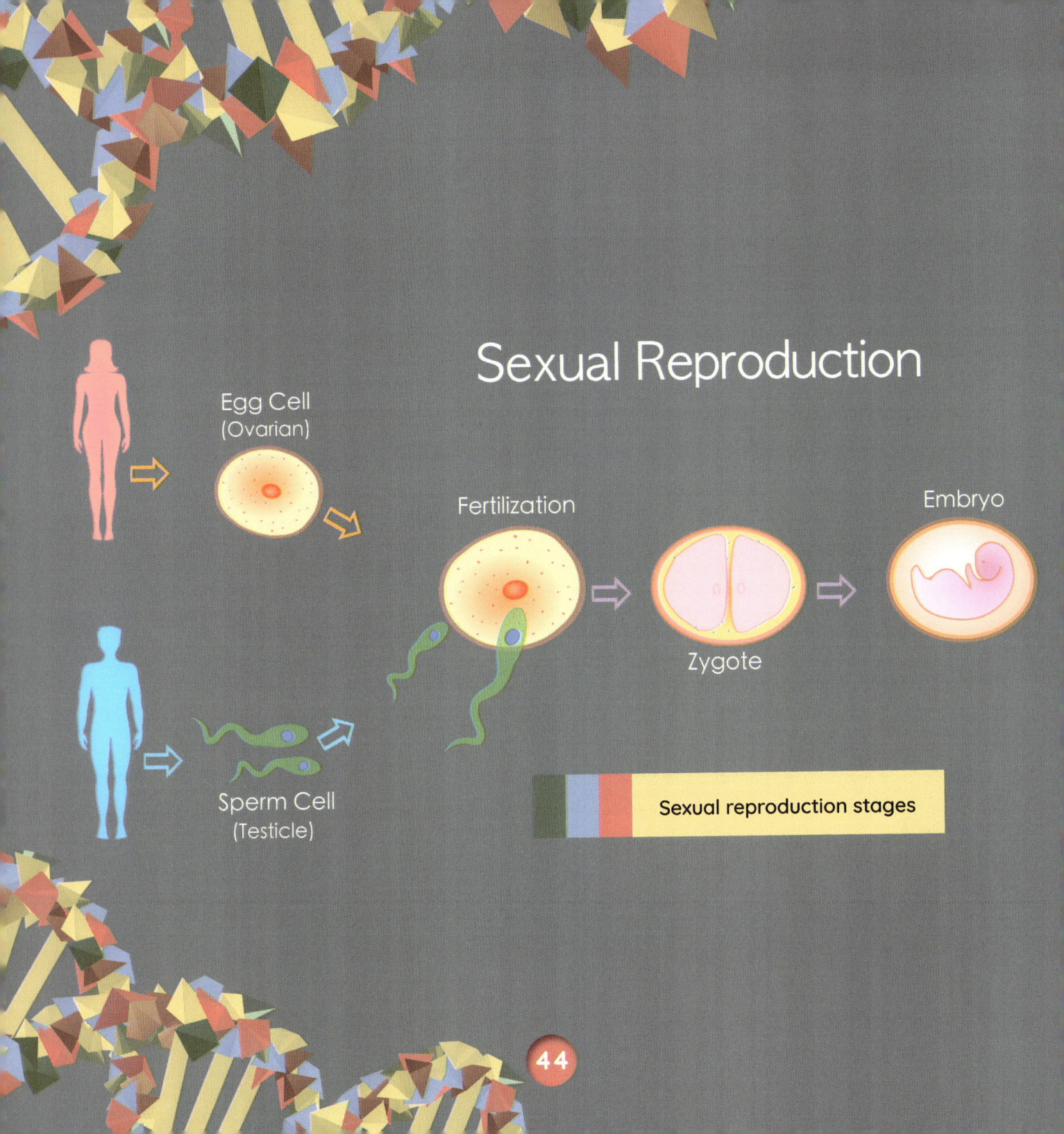

Sexual Reproduction

Egg Cell (Ovarian)

Sperm Cell (Testicle)

Fertilization

Zygote

Embryo

Sexual reproduction stages

Sexual reproduction is reproduction where sex cells of male and female combine to create a new life. Fertilization happens when a sperm cell and an egg cell unite. The fertilized egg is called a zygote. The zygote divides and grows and develops. Eventually, the new organism will become fully mature.

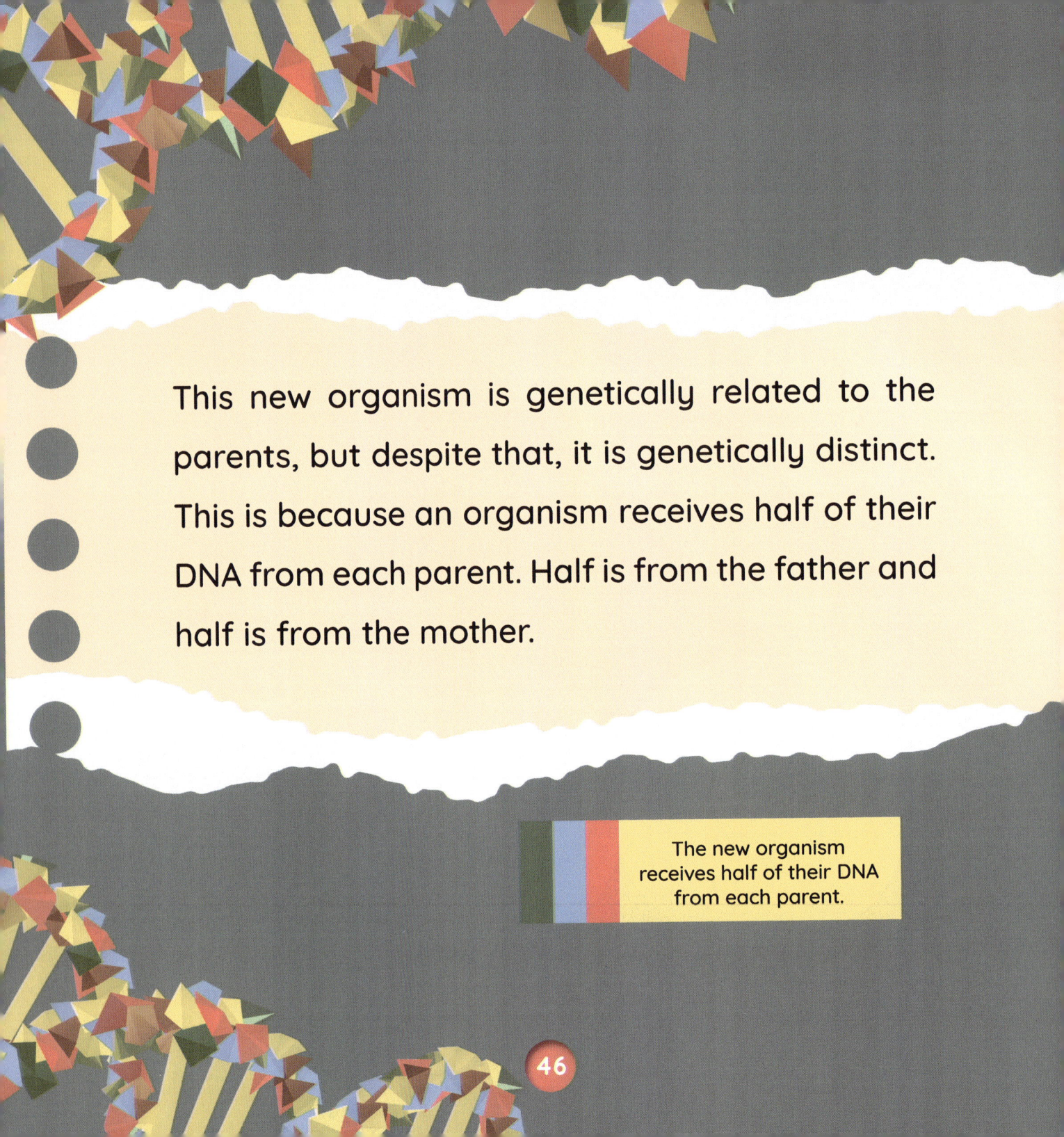

This new organism is genetically related to the parents, but despite that, it is genetically distinct. This is because an organism receives half of their DNA from each parent. Half is from the father and half is from the mother.

The new organism receives half of their DNA from each parent.

½ Father

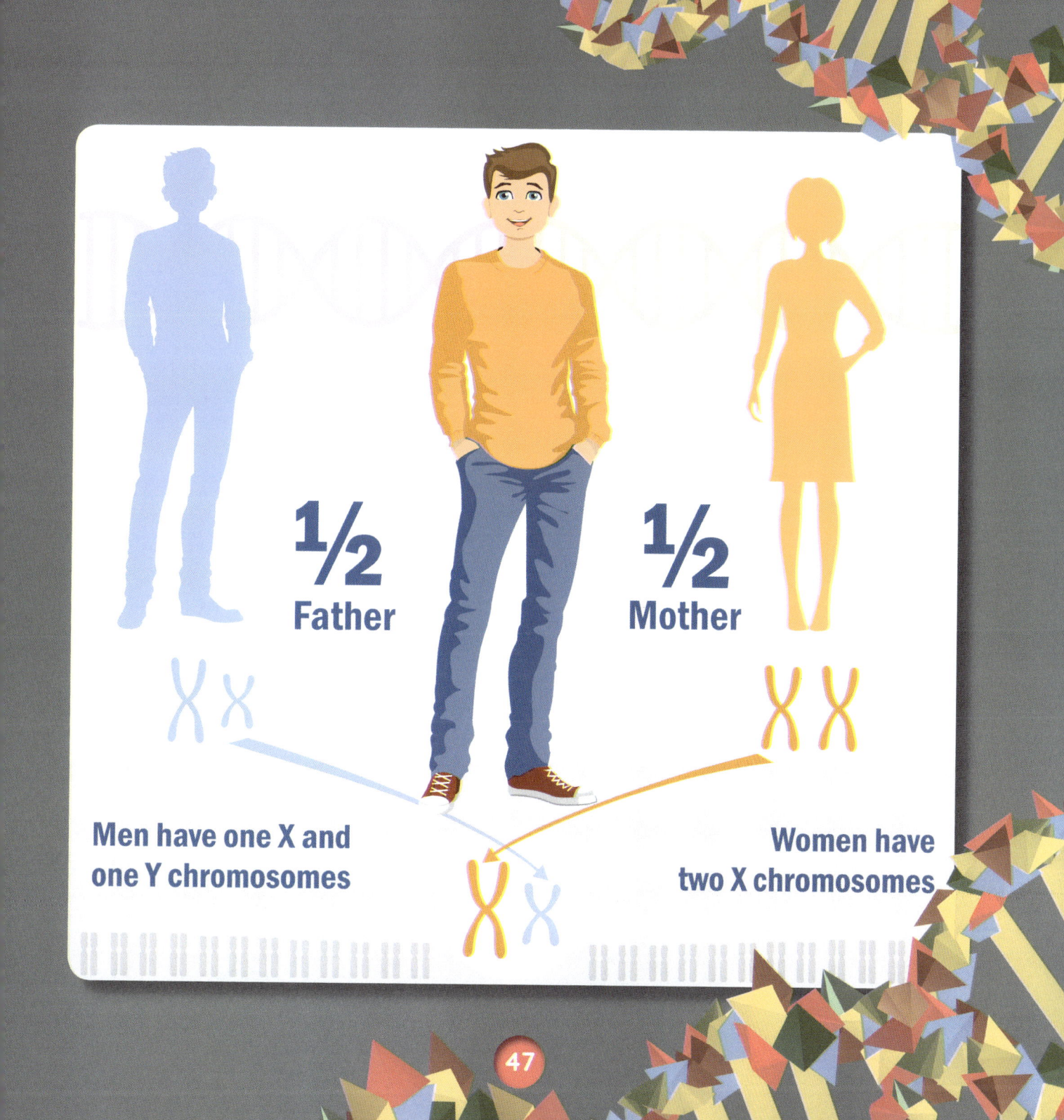

½ Mother

Men have one X and one Y chromosomes

Women have two X chromosomes

47

Eye color

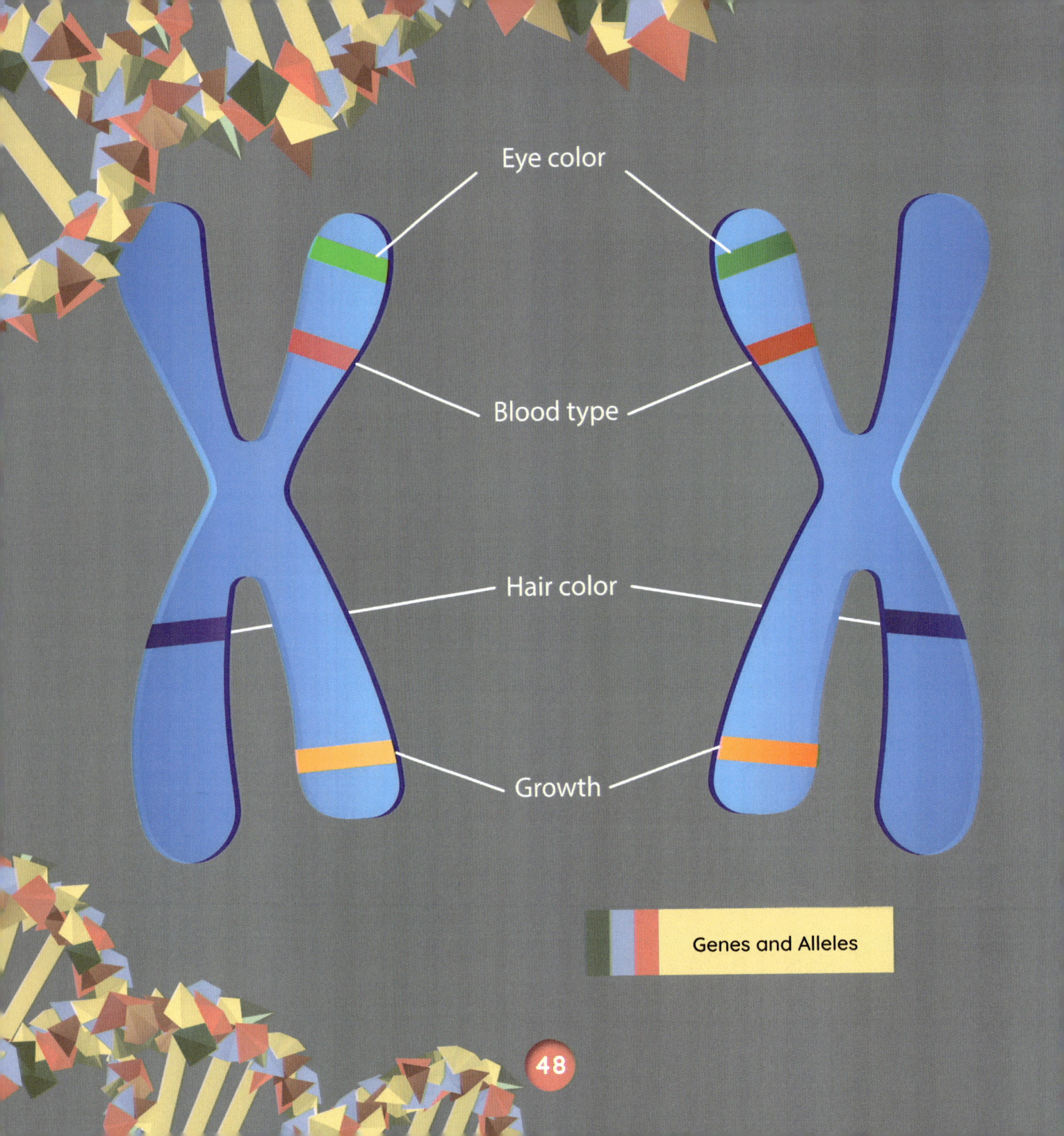

Blood type

Hair color

Growth

Genes and Alleles

Some alleles are dominant and some are recessive. Since we get DNA from both parents, we have two sets of both genes. The dominant alleles for those genes will get expressed. Recessive alleles will only be expressed if there are no dominant alleles for that gene.

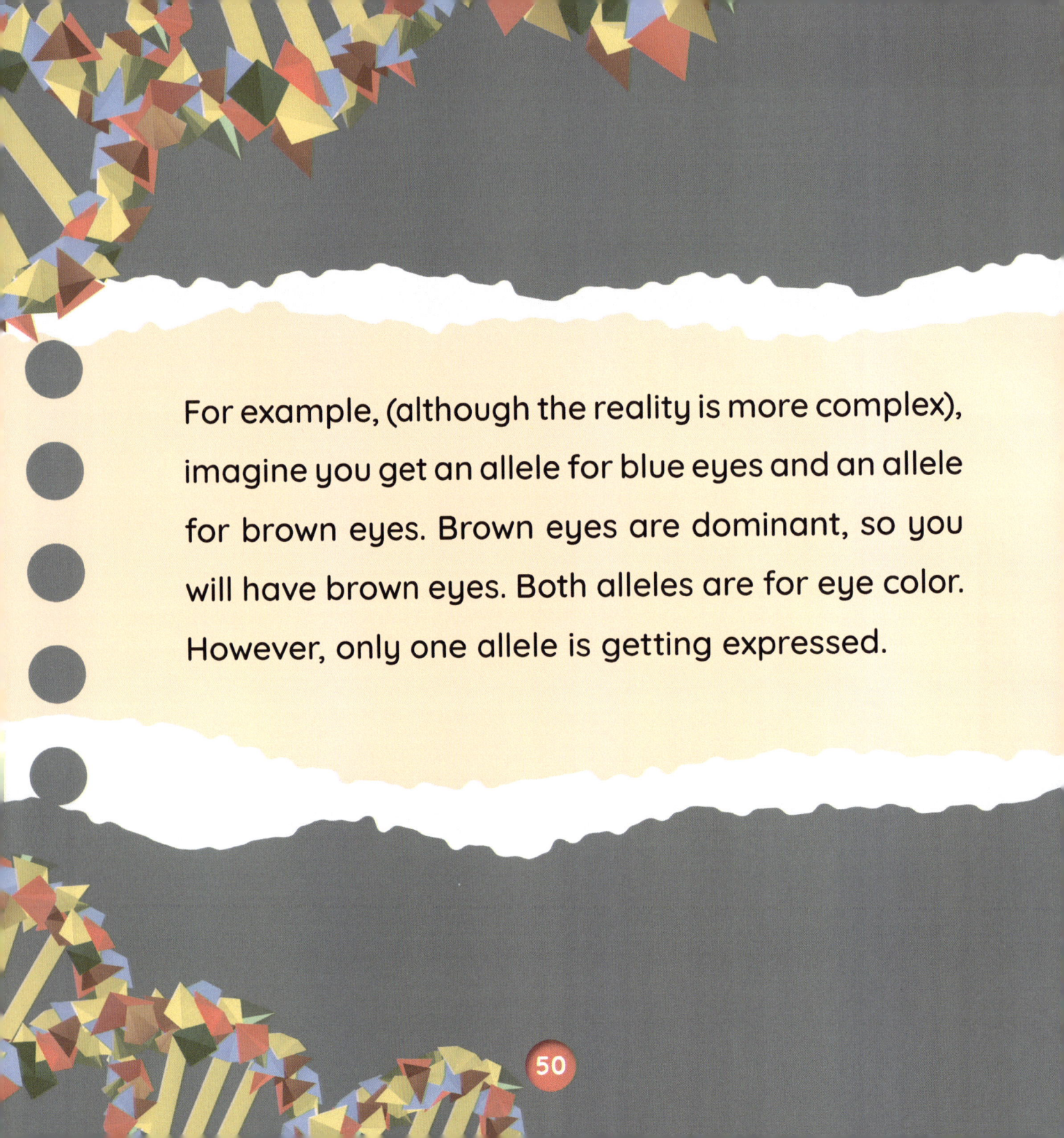

For example, (although the reality is more complex), imagine you get an allele for blue eyes and an allele for brown eyes. Brown eyes are dominant, so you will have brown eyes. Both alleles are for eye color. However, only one allele is getting expressed.

	b	b
B	Bb	Bb
B	Bb	Bb

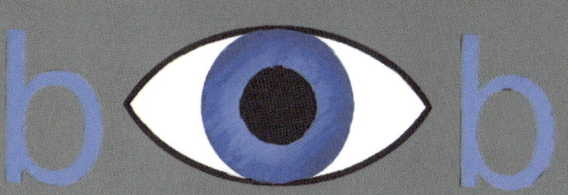

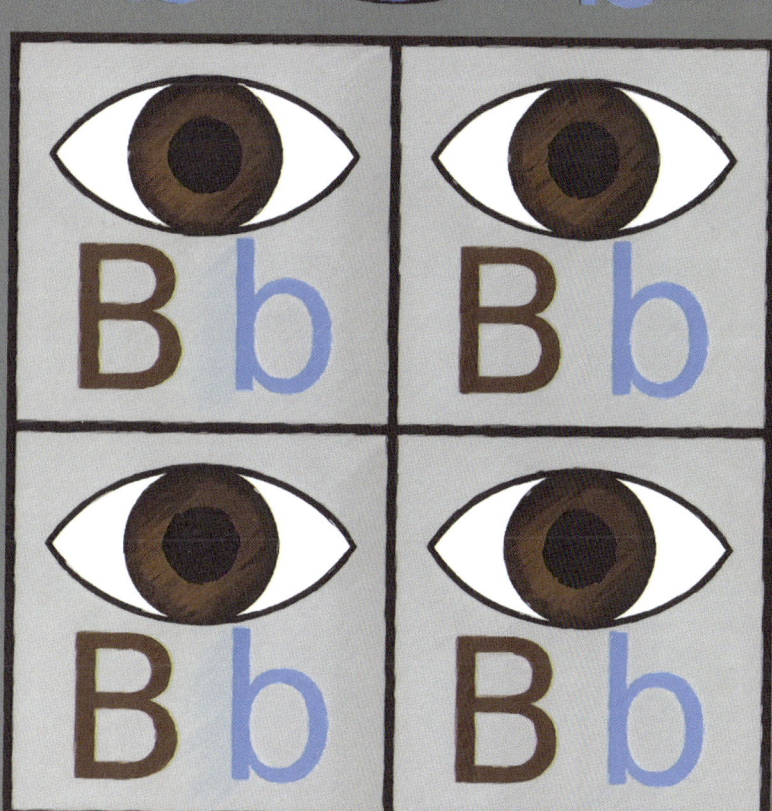

If one parent has blue eyes and the other has brown eyes then all the children will have brown eyes but will carry a blue allele so their children could have blue eyes

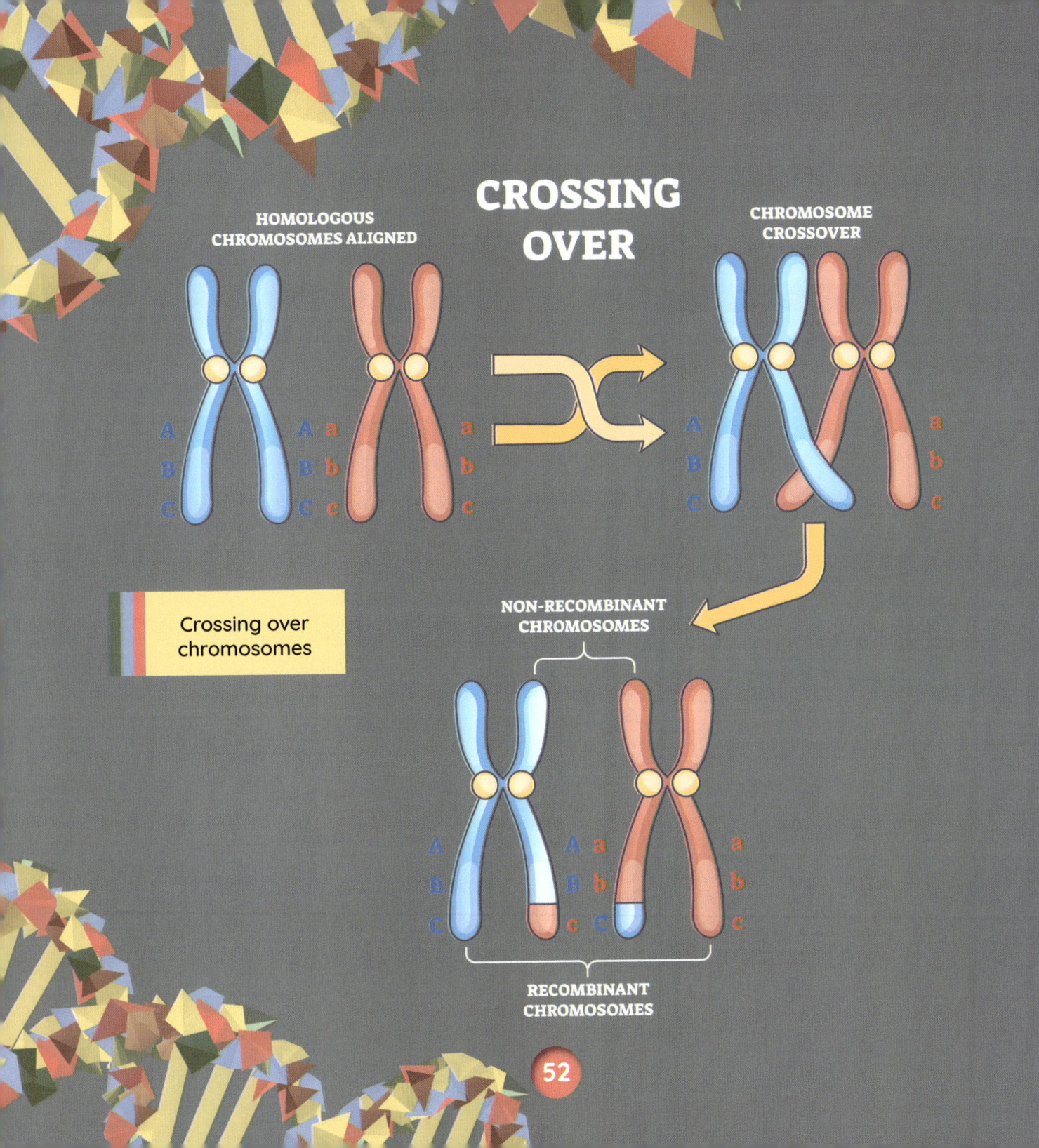

CROSSING OVER

HOMOLOGOUS CHROMOSOMES ALIGNED

A   A a   a
B   B b   b
C   C c   c

CHROMOSOME CROSSOVER

A   a
B   b
C   c

Crossing over chromosomes

NON-RECOMBINANT CHROMOSOMES

A   A a   a
B   B b   b
C   C c   c

RECOMBINANT CHROMOSOMES

During crossing over, alleles are exchanged. This means a recessive gene from a parent can get passed on to a child. This recessive gene might not be expressed in the parent. However, because of meiosis, this gene might be expressed in the offspring. As a result, crossing over can help with genetic diversity.

Asexual Reproduction

Another form of reproduction is asexual. This form of reproduction does not require meiosis. Only one parent is needed and the offspring will have identical DNA as a result.

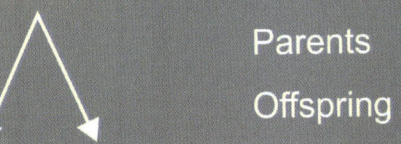

Asexual Reproduction

Parents
Offspring

In asexual reproduction, one parent can have multiple identical offspring.

BINARY FISSION

Binary fission process

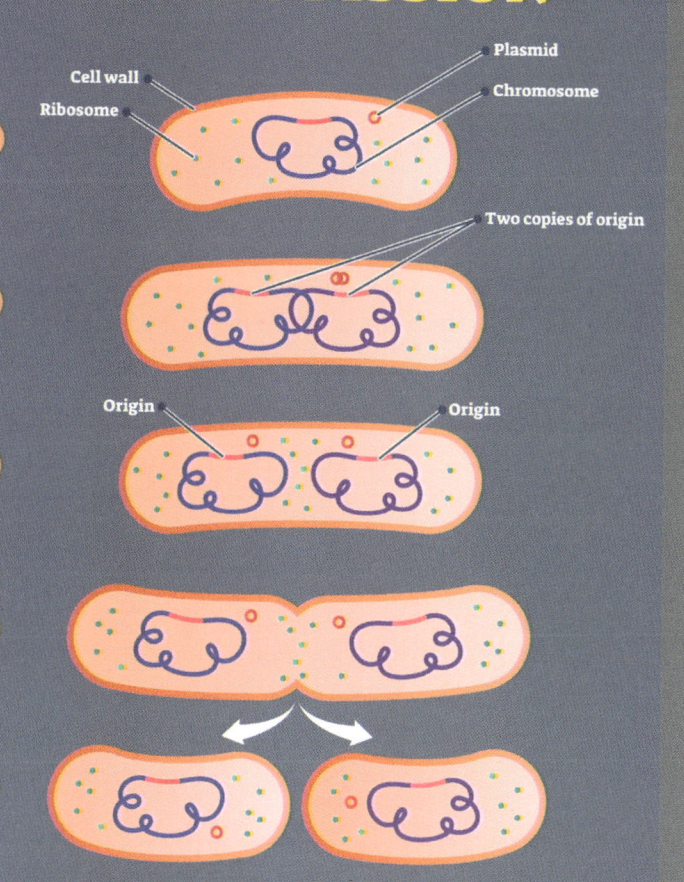

- Cell wall
- Ribosome
- Plasmid
- Chromosome
- Two copies of origin
- Origin
- Origin

There are many ways asexual reproduction can occur. One way is binary fission. This is when single-celled organisms reproduce. This happens in prokaryotes and is quite similar to mitosis. However, since prokaryotes do not have a nucleus the process has some differences.

Asexual Reproduction

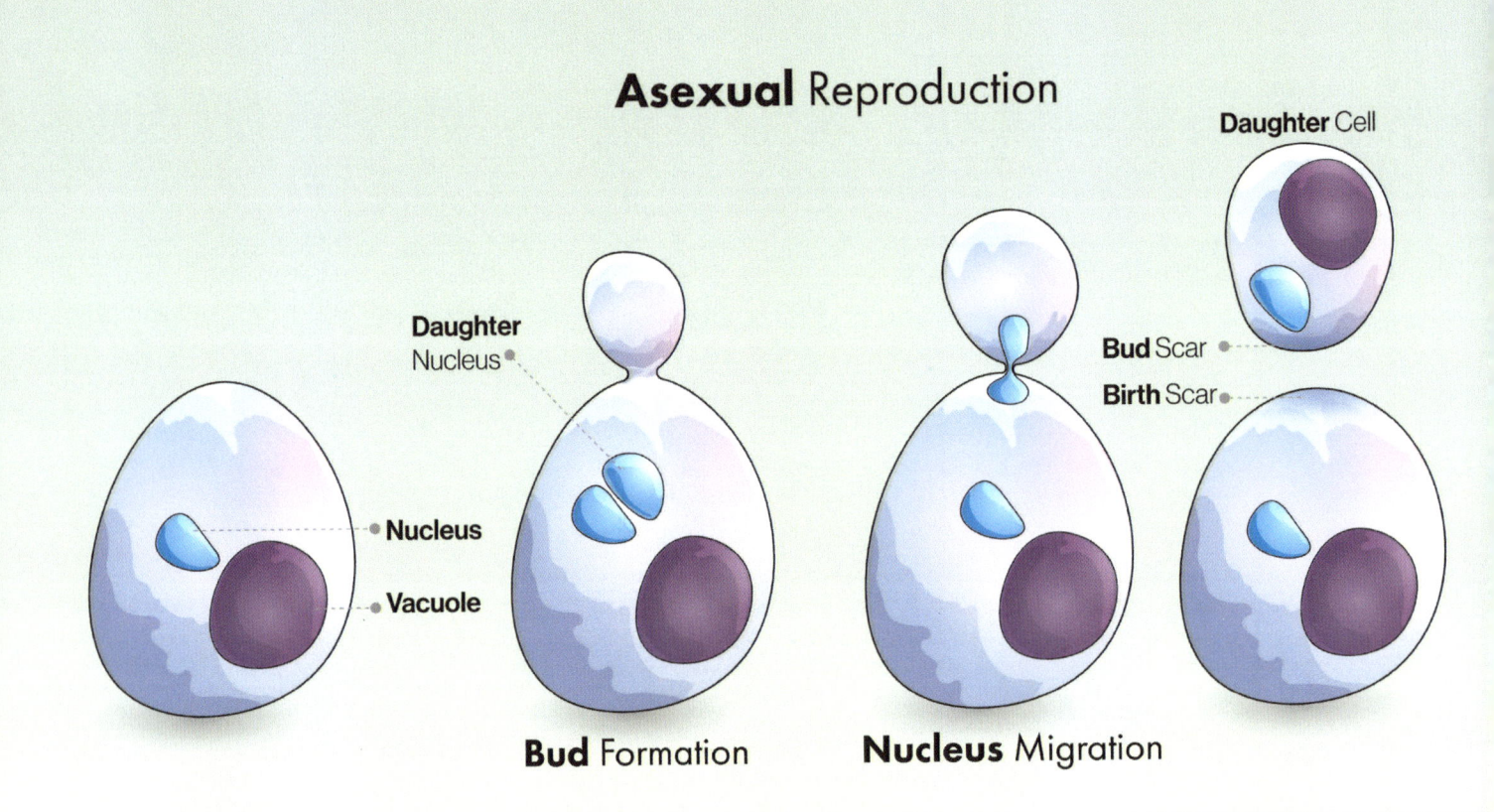

- Daughter Nucleus
- Nucleus
- Vacuole
- **Bud** Formation
- **Nucleus** Migration
- Daughter Cell
- Bud Scar
- Birth Scar

BUDDING in YEAST

Another way is through budding. This is when a part of an organism undergoes mitosis to produce a bud. This bud eventually develops into a mature organism and will separate from the parent. In rare cases, no separation will occur at all.

There is also fragmentation. This is when pieces of an organism can regenerate missing parts. The result is a new individual. For example, an organism might lose a tail. That tail can then regenerate the front half of the body.

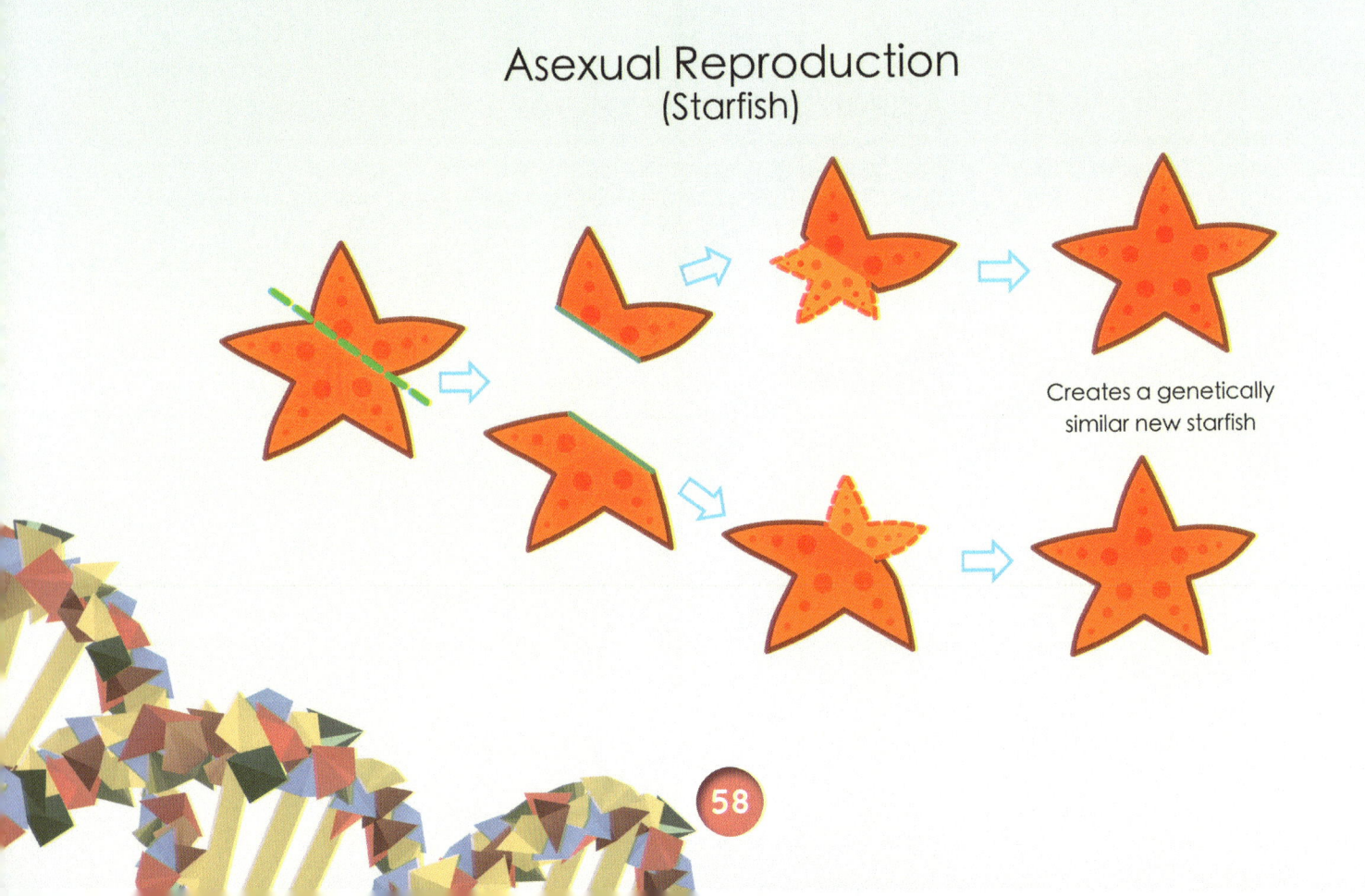

Asexual Reproduction
(Starfish)

Creates a genetically similar new starfish

Axolotl Limb Regeneration

A	B	C	D		
Intact	Trauma	Wound-healing	Blastema formation	Re-differentiation	Re-development

Skin
Bone
Cartilage
Muscle
Stem cells

Axolotl limbs go through a multi-stage process, from injury to regenerating the lost appendage

This kind of reproduction should not be confused with limb regeneration. Some species can regenerate limbs they have lost. This is not reproduction since it does not result in a new organism.

Advantages and Disadvantages of Sexual and Asexual Reproduction

Sexual reproduction has some advantages over asexual reproduction. Meiosis guarantees genetic variation. This means that there are more differences between individuals of the same species. Species that reproduce sexually are more likely to survive changes in the environment.

Sexual Reproduction

Meiosis

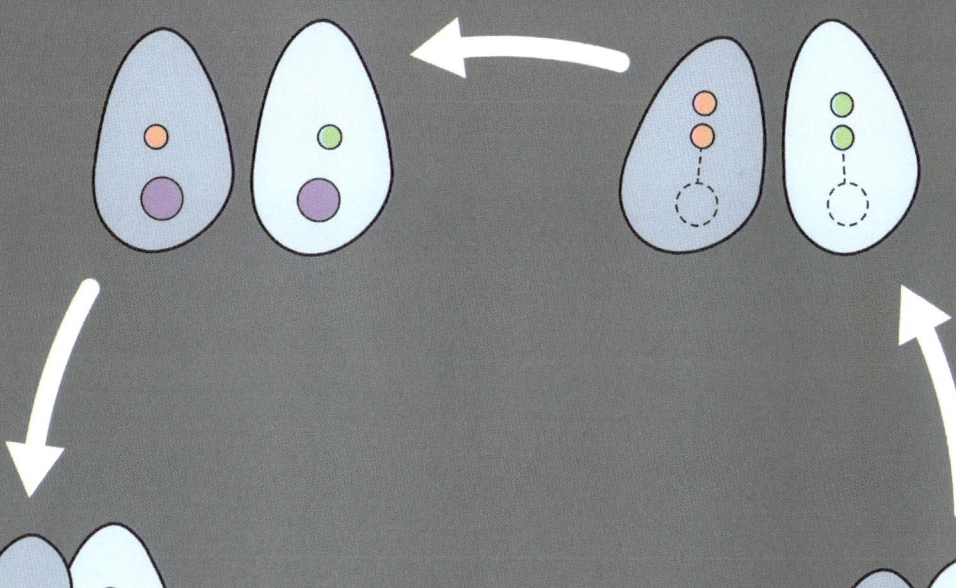

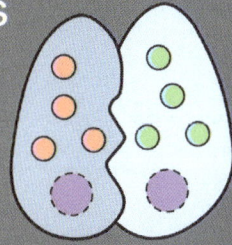

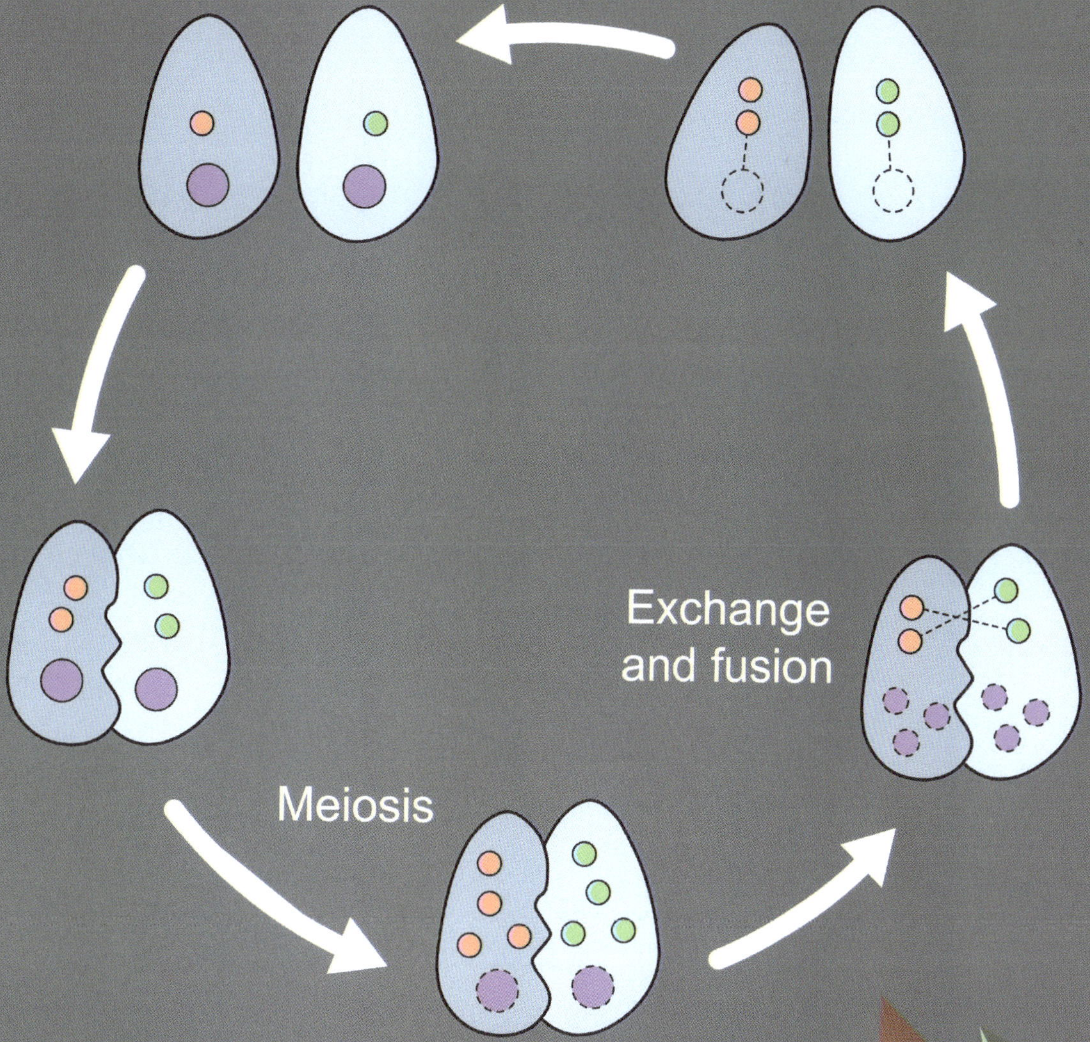

Exchange and fusion

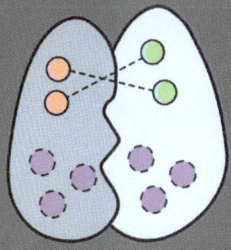

Asexual Reproduction

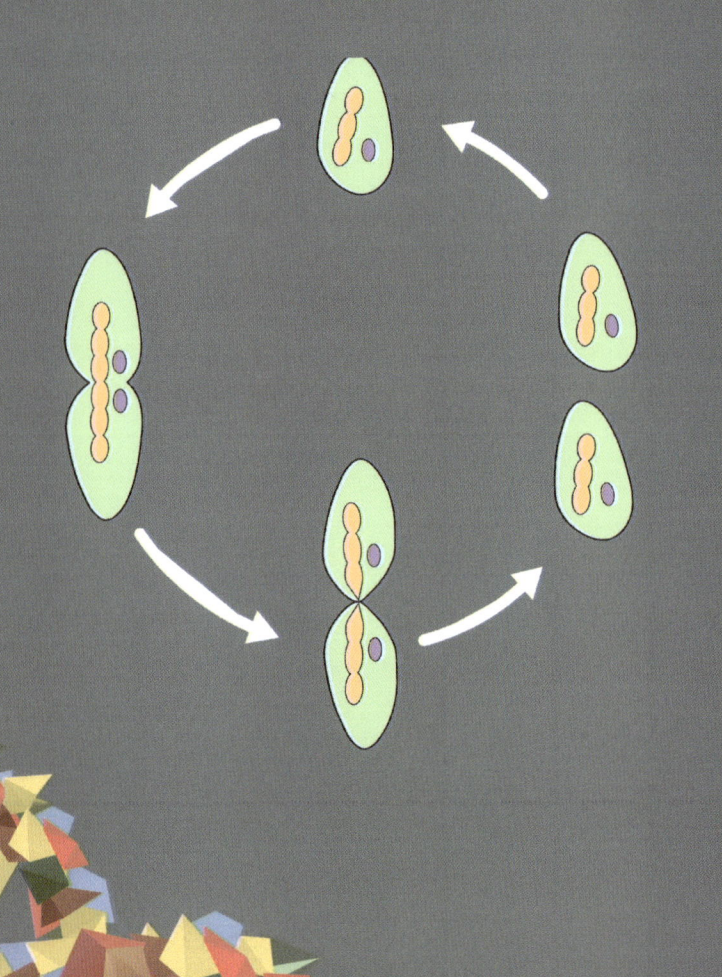

Asexual reproduction does not have this adaptability. This might be a problem if, for example, a disease were to spread rapidly in a population. If there were more genetic variations, some organisms might have traits that would allow them to survive. If not, that population could go extinct!

There are some disadvantages to sexual reproduction though. Sexual reproduction requires more energy. It can be hard to find a mate to have offspring with. Asexual reproduction, on the other hand, takes less energy and only requires one parent.

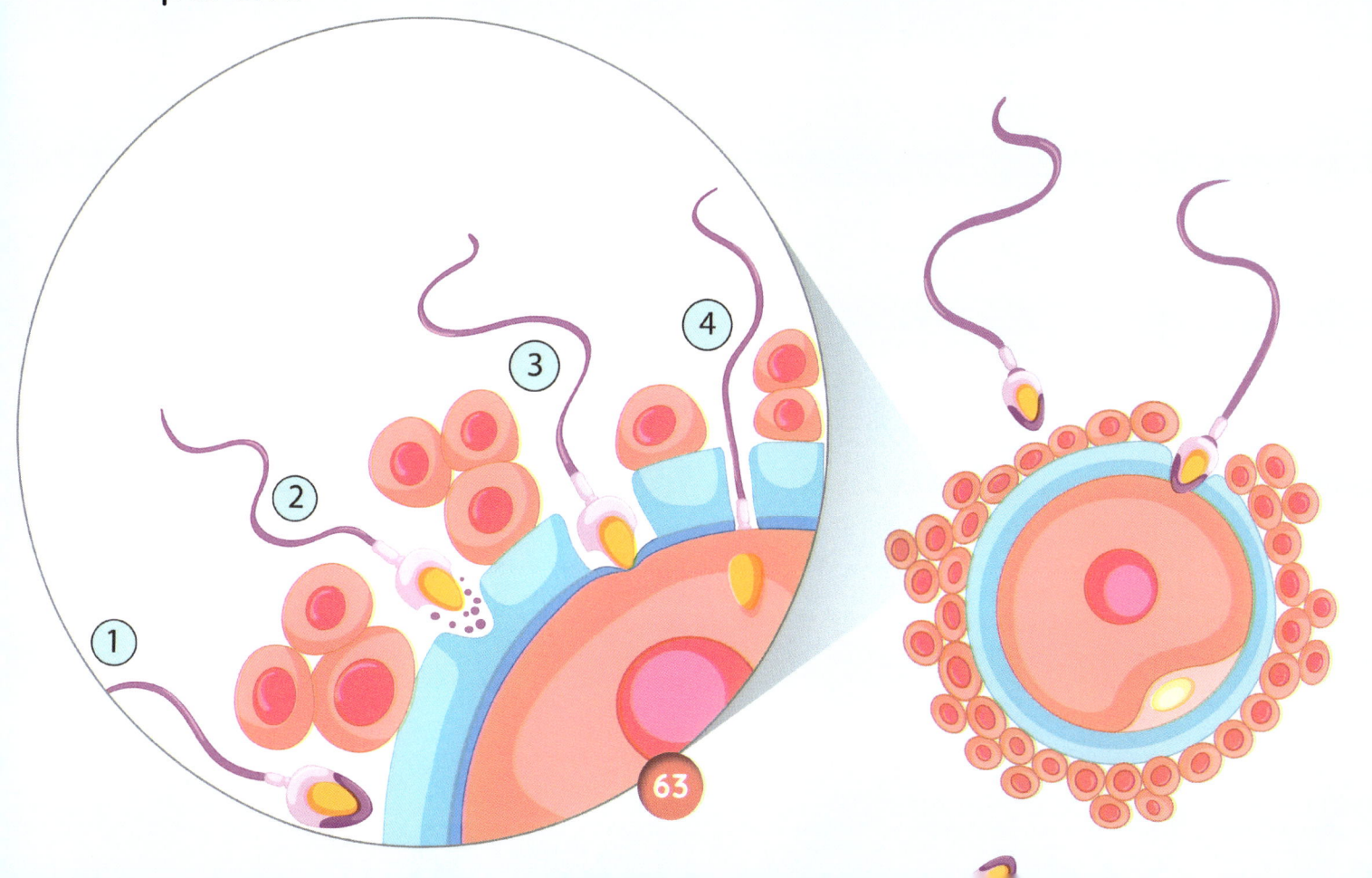

Bonus Content
Punnett Squares

Punnett squares can help people calculate the odds a specific trait will be passed on. Each parent possesses two alleles for one gene. These can be the same allele or different. Only one can get passed down. The other allele will be supplied by the other parent.

A diagram showing typical test crosses and the potential outcomes

PUNNETT SQUARE

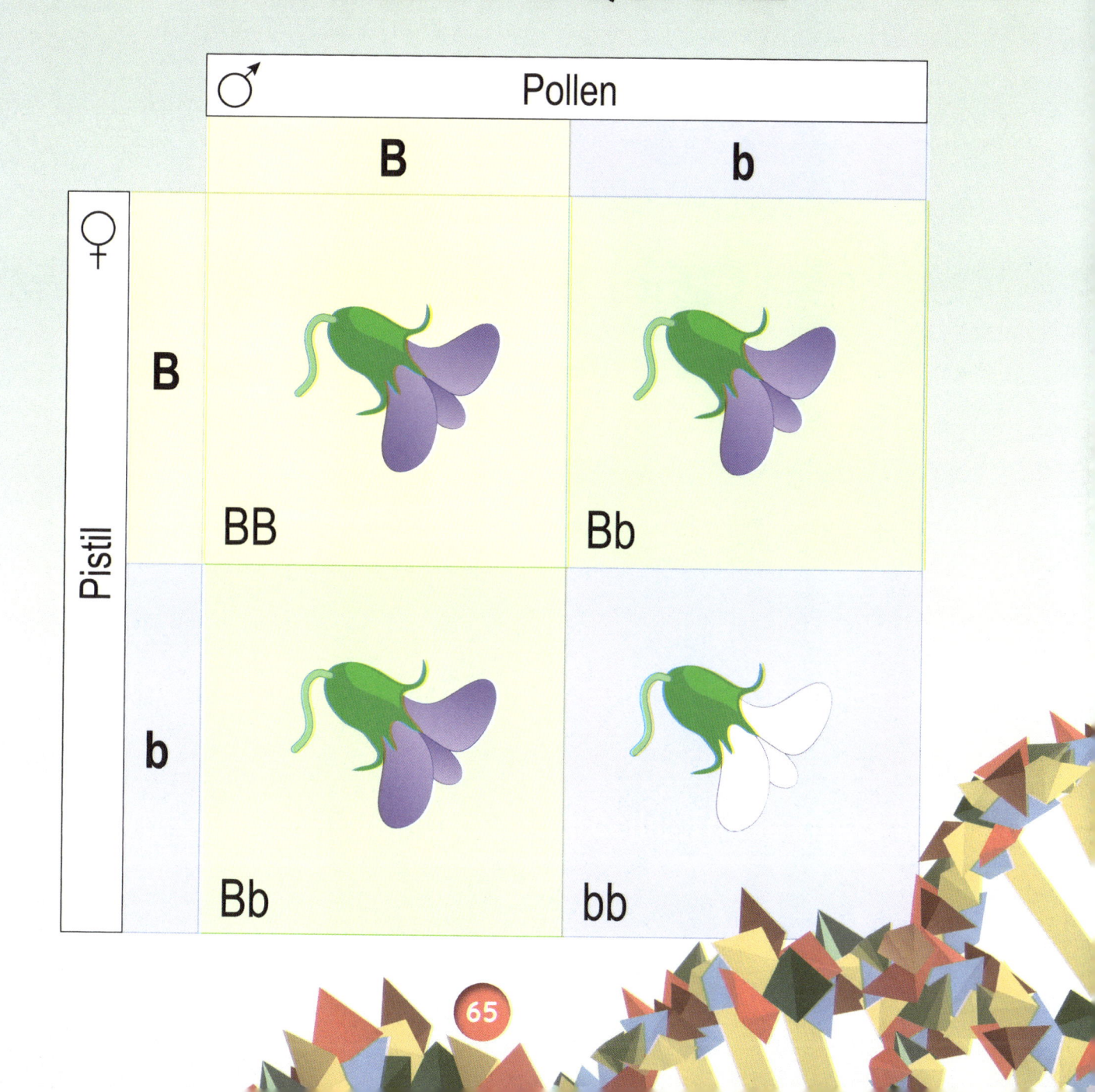

	♂ Pollen	
	B	**b**
♀ Pistil **B**	BB	Bb
b	Bb	bb

Punnett squares represent alleles with letters. A capital letter is dominant. A lower case letter is recessive. For example, B is for brown eyes, and it is dominant. Blue eyes are recessive and noted with a b.

	B	b
B	BB	Bb
b	Bb	bb

B for brown eyes; b for blue eyes

Parents | Baby's eye color

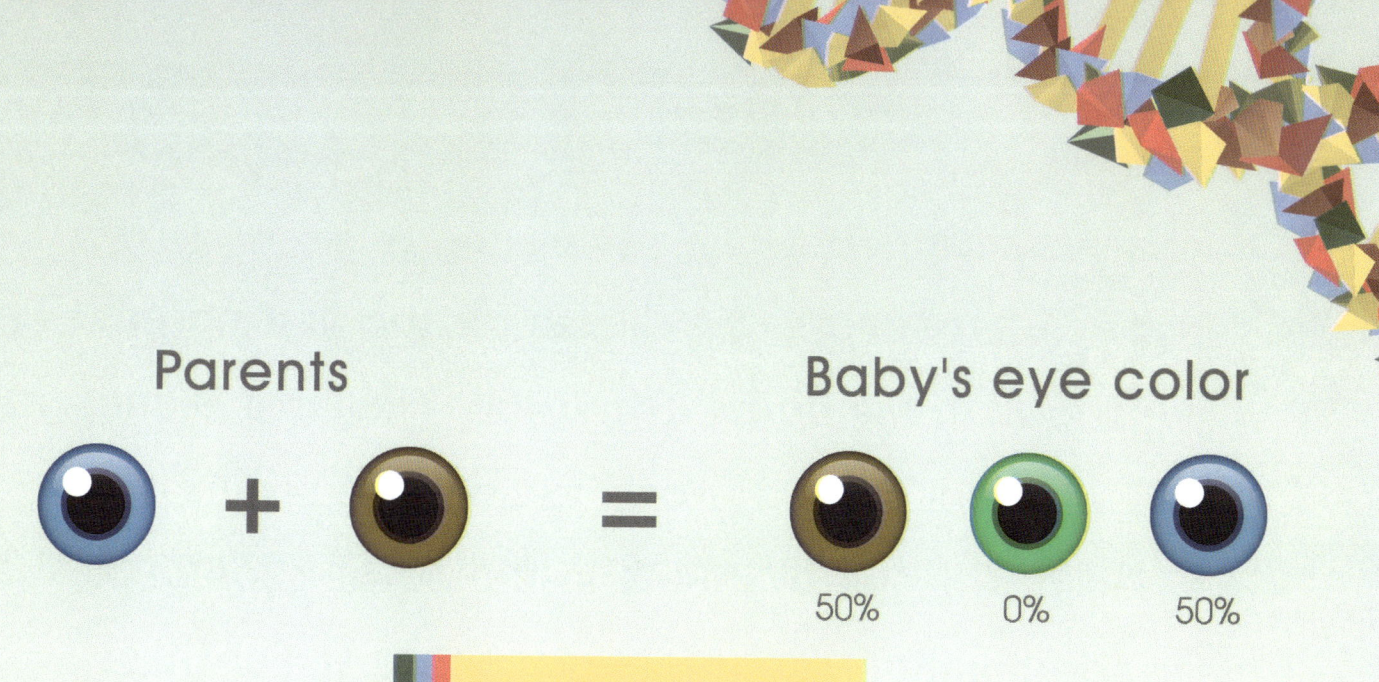

🔵 + 🟤 = 🟤 🟢 🔵
           50% 0% 50%

Baby eye color predictor

Imagine one parent has the alleles for both brown and blue eyes. The other parent only has the alleles for blue eyes. There is a 50/50 chance which of the alleles will be inherited. It is the combination that affects what traits will be expressed.

In a Punnett square, the alleles for the first parent are shown in the boxes at the top. They are B and b. The second parent is on the side. The alleles are b and b. The combinations in the boxes represent the combinations the offspring might get. For these parents, the Punnett square shows 50% with Brown eyes and 50% with blue eyes. These parents have a 50/50 chance of having a child with brown or blue eyes.

	B	b
b	Bb	bb
b	Bb	bb

Multicellular organisms are made up of somatic cells and sex cells. Sex cells are also called gametes. Gametes are produced during meiosis. This is a form of cell division that results in four haploid cells. This kind of cell division goes through prophase, metaphase, anaphase, and telophase. However, these processes happen twice over two stages. There is also crossing over to exchange genetic material between chromosomes.

The result is four, genetically distinct, haploid daughter cells. Haploid means that the cells have half of the number of chromosomes needed for that species. Being haploid, the male and female sex cells can combine to create a zygote. This is a new life. The zygote develops into maturity. Sexual reproduction can be advantageous because it results in more genetic variation in a species.

Visit

www.speedypublishing.com

To view and download free content on your favorite subject and browse our catalog of new and exciting books for readers of all ages.

Printed in Great Britain
by Amazon